D1605816

God Present as Mystery

God Present as Mystery

A Search for Personal Meaning
in Contemporary Theology

by
JAMES H. EBNER

ST. MARY'S COLLEGE PRESS, Winona, Minnesota

The research on which this book is based was made possible by grants from the Arthur J. Schmitt Foundation of Chicago and from The 1957 Charity Trust of Philadelphia.

Cover design and photo by Roderick Robertson, FSC

ISBN 0-88489-084-8

Library of Congress Catalog Card Number: 76-13750

Contents

Foreword

In his pilgrimage through the newer Catholic theological work, James Ebner has discovered that far from being a threat to faith the work of the scripture scholars and the philosophical writers like Rahner and Baum are a strong positive asset to both faith and religious reflection in the world in which we find ourselves. Such authors, unlike Bishop Robinson in his *Honest to God*, do not "water down" Christian truth to make it acceptable in the modern world but rather present in terms which contemporary humans can understand precisely the matters which are appropriate for the leap of faith and the reasons why the leap is anything but irrational.

It is surprising that many others have not made the same discovery that Ebner has. Both on the left and the right there seems to be a strange notion that the newer theology destroys the traditional faith. The right is threatened by such theology because it sees in it an attack on faith. The left is delighted by it because it sees in it a liberation from the former demands of faith. But in truth, the God of Karl Rahner or Gregory Baum, the Jesus of Reginald Fuller or Bruce Vawter are no less mysterious, no more "scientific," no less a matter for the faith leap than the God and the Jesus of more traditional theological presentations. And they are, for many contemporary humans at any rate, much more attractive.

Instead of being a threat, the newer theologians are one of the best resources the contemporary Church has at its disposal. The catechetical and homiletic implications, for example, of David Tracy's monumental *Blessed Rage for Order* are immense. But the newer theology is still a threat and a puzzle even to most concerned and literate Catholics.

I suspect that much of the reason has to do with language — by which I mean both vocabulary and thought categories. The letters to the *National Catholic Reporter* when Ebner's series first appeared made it clear that both the shallow left and right were unable to cope with the very different religious language Ebner was using. Those on the right thought it was an attack on faith, those on the left a dispensation from the need of faith. In both cases, there was a confusion between traditional theological language and traditional religious faith. I find this confusion hard to understand, even though I am aware of how much emphasis was put on language in older catechetical methods. There seems to be an almost irrational need to maintain language forms in defense of the faith even though the language no longer conveys what it did when it first came into religious vocabulary. A classic example is the word "person," which means today almost exactly the opposite of what it meant when it was used during the christological controversies; yet on both the right and the left the word "person" has been identified with the essence of faith in both God and Jesus. One is forced to conclude that there are personality needs being served by such rigidity of language that have nothing to do with authentic religious reflection.

But if many Catholics are comfortable with the old language and if many others are comfortable with doing nothing more than denying the old language, there are still a large number who are more troubled by meaning than they are by language and who find in the newer theological language a path to religious meaning they could not find with the old language—a meaning that is thoroughly orthodox, however unusual it may sound at first. It is for members of this third group—actual and potential—that Ebner has written this account of his theological explorations. For those who find it useful—and I think there will be many— let them use it; for those who don't know what to make of it, I would suggest that they have the humility to tolerate different language than their own without denying either faith or orthodoxy to those who arrive at God through different though parallel paths.

One of the merits of Ebner's work, it seems to me, is that it makes very clear that one cannot grasp the meaning of the newer theological emphases on a Sunday afternoon's reading or by taking a summer course. Coping with Karl Rahner, to say nothing of Bernard Lonergan, is demanding, intellectual work—the kind of work which in the present intellectually flabby state of the American church is distasteful to large numbers. It is much easier to quote Rahner as one heard last summer institute's teachers quote him instead of actually reading his works. Or as one priest complained to me of Tracy's book, "He's hard going." To which I replied, "You haven't seen anything yet. Wait until the next book." Ebner has worked long and hard; those who wish to follow him or accompany him on his pilgrimage must be prepared to do the same.

I am perhaps more optimistic than he about the possibility of an authentic American Catholic theology in the relatively near future. (It will certainly not be a "liberation" theology.) As long as American Catholics persist in reflecting on what they think is the meaning of other people's religious experience instead of on the meaning of their own, however, our contribution to the world theological discussion will be second or third rate. The basic American Catholic religious experience, it seems to me, is a combination of the experience of nativist prejudice on the one hand and political freedom on the other. You could call it a "theology of immigration" or a "theology of ethnicity," although I would prefer to call it a "theology of the precinct or of the neighborhood." In certain dark and quiet corners even now, the rich vein of that experience is being mined by such writers as David Tracy, John Shea, John Coleman, and Mary G. Durkin. Perhaps Dr. Ebner's next pilgrimage will follow such paths. And if it is not a path to home exactly, it will still be one through the old neighborhood.

Reverend Andrew M. Greeley
Holy Thursday 1976

Prologue

W<small>HY BOTHER</small> any longer with the institutional church?" an increasing number of people seem to ask. Among these are serious and genuinely religious young people. Then there are others, many of them older church-members, who are confused and frustrated: "Is everything going down the drain? Even the clergy no longer seem clear on what's wrong and what's right."

As a born Catholic I also felt the weight of such problems. For example, I became painfully aware of the conflict between the Genesis story of man and the evolutionary view. No scientific account leaves room for a single perfect human pair at the start of the race. Scripture experts, for their part, insist that the passages about Adam were not meant to be factual reports. Yet if there was no first male named Adam, then what happens to original sin and all that hangs on it—Calvary, redemption, infant baptism?

Moreover, having made a career of teaching, I felt under pressure to have answers for others also. Finally I left the classroom to study theology, earning a master's degree in New York City after nearly two years of courses.

But I realized that I had only begun. So I applied to private foundations and secured sixteen thousand dollars, which carried me through four years of full-time study in

11

Washington, D.C., and in Cambridge, England. Yet even though I completed a doctorate recently, I have, of course, not found the answers I had expected. I know that it sounds foolish the moment it is put into words, but I had vaguely assumed that there could be clear-cut solutions to religious problems, that somewhere there must be a map room or a control center. After all, there are thousands of books in theological libraries. I felt that surely somebody must know.

Well, today I understand how nobody on earth has the answers, neither pope nor theologian. No human being can claim to share God's mind. No one can say for sure what God's will is in any particular situation.

Nevertheless, I have not searched for six years in vain. Contemporary theology, despite its generally bad name, can be both liberating and nourishing. As a teacher I have been able to observe what theology can do for people. I have been with groups as they went through selected readings from Baum, Dulles, Rahner, and others. Once we had become acquainted and could react spontaneously, it became clear that we were at something really worthwhile. Particularly significant were occasional comments like, "I've been convinced of this for a long while but didn't think it proper to say so." Ultimately the enthusiastic responses of students encouraged me to put down on paper a summary of my findings.

But to say that contemporary theology can be hopeful and constructive is not to claim that this book effectively transmits the good news. The basic religious issues are raised here, however, and some positive direction is pointed out, so that if these chapters are used as a takeoff for group discussion, good things should happen. The book's usefulness may lie less in telling or reporting than in inviting others to consult their own experience.

The leading motif of this book is God, whom we will refer to generally as Mystery Present, for this reason: the term "*God*" is so familiar to us that it may not challenge us to rethink what we believe. Whereas *Mystery* stresses the silence and invisibility of the Ultimate that is also unlimited and undecipherable. The Ultimate we may also experience as overwhelmingly "Present," as an unspeaking person in a dark room may be really present to us. The phrase "Mystery Present" has the added advantage of hinting that God is beyond the limitations of a human person.

The overall orientation of the book, with Mystery Present as the integrating insight, could be classified as personalist and existentialist.* Yet in these chapters I do not attempt a systematic treatment of the personalist model, nor of any of the theologies that I learned from. I am content to let the reflections remain more or less eclectic, chosen from various authors and various contexts, with no great effort to bring about internal consistency. To achieve what unity there is in the book, I may have selected narrowly and cited authors as if they were in harmonious agreement when, in fact, their views and methods are widely divergent. Add to all that the chances of shortsighted reading and plain misunderstanding on my part. But these are risks worth running. My aim here is less to present an academically well-rounded survey than to report what I have found helpful for myself thus far, while remaining open to correctives and to better views. Clearly I am not proposing some new dogmatism to substitute for some old dogmatism.

In conducting my education in public like this, however, I do not feel presumptuous. I am convinced that others like myself are going through a therapeutic phase in their religious development. I am not concerned whether anyone looking for answers is going to settle for mine, but I do hope that my searching will encourage others to search.

To try stating the point of the book in one paragraph, I would say this: despite the cruelty and absurdity of life, we are immeasurably important and blessed, no matter what our job and salary, no matter what our attainments or lack of them. Who we really are and what we amount to is dramatized by the Father's work in the dead Jesus. God the Unknown Father is present to each of us, if only we attend to our depths. Within us we have the most profound resources, for the kingdom that Jesus came to preach is already begun among us. Divine love energy flows through the universe, causing us not simply to be but also to reach out. The very meaning of creation is the formation of brotherhood in response to the lure of Mystery Present. To believe and to be saved is to appreciate ourselves, to care about one another, to be open to Mystery.

NOTE

*The Epilogue describes this category of theology with regard to other important types. On the Tracy scale, this position seems to fall under the "neo-orthodoxy" model. See David Tracy, *Blessed Rage for Order: The New Pluralism in Theology* (New York: Seabury Press, 1975), pp. 27-31.

1 Change and Doubt

To GET into the discussion with a minimum of introduction, we could ask the question: what do we think we are doing when we talk theology? Whether among professionals or among ourselves, we could say that *to theologize is to reflect upon what we believe.* The implications which follow from this statement are important, and perhaps startling.

SIGNBOARDS TO MYSTERY

To begin with, theology is about what we do not actually know since faith is a commitment to what we cannot inspect as a fact. Even at its most systematic, conducted by experts, theology is a logical and consistent effort to arrange signboards pointing into the velvety blackness — or into the blinding light.

This root truth we readily slide over, because of our facility with words in Western culture. Because we have the words for holy things, we too often feel that we have them under some kind of control. Thanks also to conditioning as children, we grew up accepting words as convincing answers to religious questions. Hence many of us have taken the matter as settled when told that Jesus is the son of God the Father. After all, everyone knows what a father is, and moreover this is a term we are familiar with from the New Testament. Today, however, we realize that "Father" and "Lord" are human images applied to what we believe but cannot put our hands on.

Theology then is reflection on what we believe. It is not about what we know as flat fact. "The content of faith," notes Avery Dulles, "is always something that we do not see and cannot strictly prove."[1] Conversely, if we know something as a fact beyond doubt, then it cannot be something we hold on faith.

A DYNAMIC ACTIVITY

A second implication is that theology is something dynamic, something one is driven to. It is the effort of believers to understand in some way what they feel compelled to embrace. To be a firm believer need not mean that one closes his eyes. In fact, if a person is critically honest, he cannot. As Dulles points out, "the life of faith consists in constant probing."[2] We cannot stop ourselves from asking questions about life and death, about good and evil — and about the rightfulness of the way we interpret and deal with them.

And a lively faith can include doubt. For "doubt is often an authentic Christian virtue."[3] Especially today, in a time of rapid change, doubt can be an important element in personal growth. Thus a priest-psychologist writes:

> Doubt cannot help but come into an individual's life when institutional Churches continue to offer interpretations of life that no longer match his own experience or knowledge. This, of course, is the cutting edge of belief itself, a profound aspect of human growth. The individual who is in touch with his experience does not readily accept

an interpretation that contradicts it, attempts to suppress it, or seems to make little of its character.[4]

In our times a believer sooner or later comes to ask the question, "How can I accept what I know cannot be true?" Astronauts, for instance, have gone into outer space and have not seen any of the angels, nor the Jesus who ascended into heaven. All right, so traditional Christian faith is clothed in mythological language. But once we begin the process of radical interpretation, where do we stop? Women, for example, no longer have to wear their hats in church. But if we no longer follow St. Paul's injunction that females must be veiled at the assembly, since we now see how that practice is conditioned by its culture, then what else is going to be culturally conditioned? What solid reality will be left to believe in?

We could perhaps take comfort in the congregational recitation of the Nicene creed in unison at the assembly. Here at last, we could think, is the Catholic faith uniformly and fully achieved. Yet when we compare notes with each other, we find that the recited words cover an unclassifiable range of understandings and dispositions. And rightly so: the Church is no factory turning out reproductions from a single mold. Rather, it is a Spirit-filled community where each encourages the other to be what he or she can. As Eugene Kennedy remarks, "Only a Church that sincerely believes in man as he is and that understands and accepts the rich texture of faith can help human beings to become true believers."[5] The label "Catholic" then must include endless varieties of believing.

With doubt being a part of the process of truly believing, the mature Christian may be among the last to grade people as believers versus nonbelievers. Since at bottom we are involved with mystery and not with words, we know that "we cannot tell, with evidential certitude, whether or not we belong in the category of true believers."[6] We can only trust that we have faith. The presumed believer deals courteously with alleged unbelievers. For when he looks into his own heart, he sees that atheism is "the constant inner temptation of the theist, as a condition of faith."[7] To theologize, then, is to reflect upon what we have decided to assent to and to live out. It is as questioning and as humble as faith itself is questioning and humble.

Taking the nonbeliever seriously is surely the stance of Vatican II,[8] which no longer saw fit to repeat the condemnations from simpler times when a more or less unified Christendom existed in Europe. Believers today confront an impressive atheistic tradition. Marxism, for instance, is a world-wide force, and a standing challenge that religion is the opiate of the people and a mascot of the rich and powerful. Marxism has not yet been effectively answered in the Third World, since not words but only deeds will count as a response. Nor can a good case be made for theism in any age, claim the Freudians; religion is what men need and therefore an illusion that they create for themselves. The mystery of evil, also, baffles modern man no less than it did Job. "How," asks Rubenstein, harking back to the six million victims of the Nazis, "can Jews believe in an omnipotent, beneficent God after Auschwitz?"[9] Indeed, how do Christians handle the question? Articulating the absurdity of life that overwhelms some people today, Camus declares: "There is but one truly serious philosophical problem, and that is suicide."[10] Reading their own hearts, then, theists today theologize with understanding of and sympathy for their unbelieving brethren.

RESONATING LANGUAGE

There is a third implication of theological reflection: it has to be in our own language, not in a foreign one. To talk to one another about what is of ultimate concern, we have to use concepts and images that penetrate and resonate. Each era, and even region, has its own set of favorite ways of expression. Note how the New Testament itself exhibits not one uniform theology but several theologies. For instance, in an earlier Jewish context the question about Jesus stressed God's action among His people: "What was *happening* in Christ?" This is the basic orientation of Paul's writings, which focus on Jesus as man who came to do the work of redemption by dying and being transformed. Whereas a later question in a Greek context asked about the nature of Jesus: "Who *was* Christ?" This is the basic orientation of John's gospel, which stresses the pre-existent Christ who came as light to reveal truth.[11]

Just as the first Christians used religious terms that spoke to them directly, so we also have to speak in our own idioms. But this ongoing cultural process creates a tension between our own needs and those rites, dogmas, and scriptures from cultures past. This tension is obvious in the Catholic Church today, which found the Reformation a traumatic experience. In reaction since then, for example, there has been censorship of printed materials and a close watch on the preciseness of statements related to morality and beliefs.

But there is a problem with stressing official formulations and with trusting in right words. For one thing, their original meaning fades with time. Hence the Bible itself cannot be taken literally as the final wording of eternal truth; it has to be reread against its various historical contexts. The most solemn of Church statements also have to be reread. Recognizing "the historical relativity of all doctrinal statements,"[12] we realize that creeds and dogmas and council statements have to be interpreted anew in each age. We have to keep reminding ourselves that what ultimately preserves the Church and gives us life are not the sacred words and the orthodox words, but the Spirit.

Contemporary theologizing, then, is both a response and a stimulus to religious living. Christian theology further interprets for our day God's work in Jesus as first proclaimed in the early Church. But then there arises the problem of change in a tradition resisting change. Perhaps one way to describe the polarization in Christian churches today is to characterize it as a struggle between those who want to think and feel in today's terms, and those who understand loyalty as clinging to familiar and traditional ways. Ours is a painful time of transition, from long-established forms to what has not yet emerged. As happens in time of cultural shift, it is the older people who feel the pain of having to adjust. And they may have no way to understand the young unaffected by tradition, for these may be "incapable of sincerely believing in the same way that their parents or grandparents did."[13]

What is going on with Catholics, however, is no mere cultural shift. What we are experiencing is the collapse of what remains not only of the immigrant American Church and of the European anti-Reformation Church, but also of the medieval Church and the Church of St. Augustine. And we are apparently watching the erosion of the tradition dating, in fact, back to Constantine, when the Roman Church was given privileged status. To take one practice that is changing, Christians in the West baptized infants shortly after birth on the assumption, sketched out by St. Augustine, that babies had sin on their souls and would be saved only through baptism. That practice was carried out unquestioned for almost fifteen hundred years. Today, however, it is no longer universally assumed that infants are born in a sinful state due to Adam's original sin. Hence there is no longer the pressure to hurry the baby to church lest it die before the sin is washed off its soul. Whether early or late, we take the child to church today with the understanding that baptism is the rite by which he or she is welcomed to the believing community.

The day is gone then, when a neat and uniform theology can be transmitted through Latin manuals distributed throughout the world. Amidst critical questioning and rediscovery, the theologizing of professionals is now diverse and changing. Everything in tradition is being restudied. Theological reflection is undergoing a profound change.

But of course it is no easy matter to die with one era and to try being reborn into another. It is understandable that many Christians fight change, especially when some familiar and beloved forms of the past are put aside for what is less lovely or satisfying. Yet here, as in much else about life, what is vital may also have to be messy and ambiguous. Whether one finds our age depressing or exciting, he can only take it as it comes. There is no ready solution. Vatican II could achieve only so much. The struggle to evolve new expressions of faith will continue to be complicated by the effort needed to be patient with one another, to discuss, and even at times to engage in conflict.

UNSPOKEN ASSUMPTIONS

Theology, like any other human reflection, entails a fourth implication: the way we express our faith will follow not only our conscious values and experiences but also our whole network of assumptions and presuppositions. This network (deep within the nervous system and thus difficult to recognize and still more difficult to question or to change) is the more or less hidden agenda of each individual, as well as of his communities and culture. We can see how a hidden agenda operates when two people get into a heated argument. Their difference may not really be over some particular conclusion; it might merely be an expression of mutual dislike or an attempt to assert one's superiority. They will make progress only when they try to explore the difference in the assumptions behind the conclusion.

In religion as in the rest of life, we have to be aware of how assumptions alter performance and thinking. It is one thing, for example, to profess a loving Father; yet another to act as if He were mainly the avenger, the angry God demanding to be placated by peace offerings and bloody sacrifices.

Coming at the confusion within Christian communities today from this angle of presuppositions, we see some people discarding assumptions that they no longer find adequate, while others hold on for dear life. For example, one could believe that human beings can somehow connect directly with the divine mind, not only with God's plan implicit as in natural law but with God's own understanding as expressed immediately and literally in the Bible. Similarly, one could assume that the Catholic Church is divine, with divinity that would endow details with almost magical power. One could assume, further, that somehow, on special occasions at least, the pope has access to divine information, beyond human study and research. An unspoken premise like this seems to lend energy to the infallibility debate. Many such assumptions about a triumphalistic Church, however, were modified by Vatican II; it proposed, instead, modest and realistic images like "People of God" and "Pilgrim Church."

Especially in a centralized, hierarchical Church, polarization would show up most sharply on the issue of Church. Those who assume, for instance, that law and order are primary and that loyalty to the old-time religion is fundamental can scarcely endure people who would read papal documents and bishops' letters more as guidelines than as divine decrees.

Contemporary theologians, of course, have their own presuppositions. They assume, for example, certain cultural values of the twentieth century — such as the dignity of man, freedom of conscience and religion. These had not been major values in classical theology. It is something really new in the Catholic Church that one of the sixteen documents of Vatican II, the *Declaration on Religious Freedom*, rests upon such freedom as an inalienable human right.

But, one may object, loyalty to Christ's Church is the real issue — not this twisting and turning to keep up with theologians of one stripe or another. Well, this common protest covers a number of assumptions. But to take the issue to be fidelity and allegiance, we could formulate this question: on the score of theological reflection, how does a Catholic show his loyalty today?

The response could be brief: if someone wants to be loyal to the hierarchy of the Church, then he or she should follow the example — and the directives — of two popes and of three thousand bishops. At Vatican II they tried to rethink traditional Catholic truth in contemporary terms. Make the changes, they said in effect, that promote living Catholic Christianity. With official leadership clearly on record for change, it is difficult to see how anyone could claim to be more Catholic than others simply because he or she maintains the worldview and the practices fostered, for example, by the Council of Trent.

To conclude, then, we have noted that theologizing is a reflection within our total worldview. It is to be as contemporary as the faith it expresses is living. And theology is reflection not on what we know but on what we believe. This last insight needs much unfolding, which we will get at in the next two chapters.

NOTES

1. Avery Dulles, *The Survival of Dogma* (Garden City: Doubleday, 1971), p. 141.

2. Ibid., p. 139.

3. Ibid., p. 138.

4. Eugene C. Kennedy, *Believing* (Garden City: Doubleday, 1973), pp. 69-70.

5. Ibid., p. 75.

6. Dulles, *The Survival of Dogma*, p. 142.

7. Karl Rahner, *Theological Investigations*, vol. 9, trans. Graham Harrison (New York: Herder and Herder, 1972), p. 141.

8. See Sections 19-21 of the *Pastoral Constitution on the Church in the Modern World*.

9. Richard L. Rubenstein, *After Auschwitz: Radical Theology and Contemporary Judaism* (Indianapolis: Bobbs-Merrill, 1966), p. 153.

10. Albert Camus, *The Myth of Sisyphus and Other Essays*, trans. Justin O'Brien (New York: Knopf, 1955), p. 3.

11. John Knox, *The Humanity and Divinity of Christ: A Study of Pattern in Christology* (Cambridge University Press, 1967), p. 57.

12. Dulles, *Survival of Dogma*, p. 173.

13. Ibid., p. 26.

2 Recovering the Sense of Mystery

WHAT HAPPENS to God in contemporary theology?

In the classical tradition of the theology manuals, the God issue seemed to be settled rather neatly.[1] The Five Ways of St. Thomas were used to prove the divine existence. There was the crucial distinction between divine existence and divine essence. Among the divine attributes was the omnipresence of a transcendent Being.

In contemporary Catholic theology, on the other hand, the tension of paradox is stretched to the utmost: Mystery is really present and indwells, yet is totally elusive and unknowable. In Rahner's phrase, He is "the incomprehensible obvious."[2] A God like this is not to be caught in a net of logical proofs. Instead, we will be convinced of divine presence because of something in our experience, clarified by words and practices of the community.

It is ironic that the classical approach, which claimed to be from God's side, was the approach that became abstract and rationalistic, losing the sense of wonder and truth and mystery. It put enormous confidence in proof and logical division. Its God was largely the God of reason and nature.

By contrast, the God of contemporary theology, identified through the experience of intimate beyondness, turns out to be the New Testament God whom no man has ever seen (John 1:18 and 6:46; 1 John 4:12 and 20), yet whom all can experience. The starting point here is human awareness, and the method is phenomenological. So much is this approach from man's side that some theologians refer to their reflections as theological anthropology.

THE CLASSICAL PRESUPPOSITION

Now in order to see more clearly what may be new and valuable about the contemporary method, it could be helpful to go back to the classical presupposition that theology could begin with a chapter on divine being, and that from God's side—as if somehow we could view the world with God's own mind. This program fit into a larger context, where revelation was literally God's word, available at least in Scripture. Such a program becomes more plausible when the verbal revelation is thought of as certified and is interpreted by church officials with an almost unrestricted infallibility.

In fact, however, neither the Bible nor the teaching Church can measure up to the assumption that men somehow can share the divine intellect. For the Bible, however it is the word of God, proves to be also the word of man. As the end product of whatever process, the Bible is thus a collection of human documents, historically conditioned, that yield their sense under ordinary literary interpretation. They record and testify to community faith. The Bible tells how some privileged people thought of themselves in relation to the Ultimate. Recent biblical research does not allow us to say that the Bible is a transcript of direct divine dictation.

Even the parts of the Bible which deal with Jesus do not report his words and deeds according to the demands of official biography today. To begin with, the actual authors of the New Testament apparently did not meet the man Jesus. Furthermore, there seems no reason to maintain, for instance, that St. Peter actually wrote two epistles: it was not uncommon for local writers to attribute their compositions to famous people. In any event, in a confected and literary way the gospels and epistles profess the faith of early Christianity. They do not attempt a modern historical portrait, with footnotes and other critical apparatus. They aim to "express what the person of Christ meant to the faith of the respective Christian communities."[3]

A Christian in our era, then, not only has a book inserted between him and the person he has a special interest in, but it is the kind of book that fails to provide a unified, sharp-edged picture. In short, "the Christian of today must realize that he has no channel or pipeline back to the historical Jesus."[4] There will never be an authorized film or tape of the man Jesus. Furthermore there is no one living likeness, only several interpretations. It is as though we see many portraits of the same person done in various styles of painting, as in a gallery, but not one is a photograph. The diversity of the portraits of Jesus in the New Testament will continue to confront Christians through the centuries, so that the "response of Christian faith must accordingly be diverse."[5] Whoever was the author of the Epistles to the Hebrews, for instance, presents Jesus as mediator between God and man, while St. Paul stresses Jesus as the Lord, but as the crucified Lord who was resurrected.

So far as its founding story is concerned, then, Christianity is anchored to a book. For "the root of Christian faith is the tandem: the Jesus of history as presented by the New Testament."[6] This means that we put our trust first in what early Christians said He said, as their way of telling who He was and what He meant to them. We do not seem to have a religion founded on words directly from heaven, nor even directly from Jesus. Christianity, of course, is not really based on words, but on the life-giving impulse of the Spirit who filled the early Church and who we trust continues to enlighten, invite, and impel us.

CHURCH TEACHING

As for sharing the divine mind through pronouncements of Church officials, even infallibility may be of little help—even if we were to accept the exaggerated view that the pope has access to divine information when he proclaims a truth infallibly. After two thousand years not one single Church statement has been proposed as infallible in the area of "morals." Even in the area of "faith," the number of infallible statements is not certain. "There is no infallible list of what the infallible teachings are."[7] The fact is, Dulles continues, that

> theologically educated Catholics have always known that the vast majority of the Church's teaching is fallible and therefore subject to error. In all the thousands of pages of encyclicals issued by the popes of the last hundred years, there is not to my knowledge a single sentence of infallible teaching.[8]

Something enduring has gone on within the Christian church that may be discussed under the category "infallible," but it is rank distortion to expect the teaching Church to be a truth machine.

Because of insuperable difficulties with its presuppositions, the classical approach cannot be said to have known God from God's side. We are left still very much on the outside of everything and, despite our careful logical reasoning, we have not made contact with something vital.

When we are rigorously honest about this situation, we could then urge with Callahan that the time has come to "drop the self-pretense" that we can talk about God-in-Himself on a lofty, super-human plane, above the anthropomorphisms and other human-model images common to mythology. For even when they claimed to proceed otherwise, theists have in fact always practiced "unrelieved anthropomorphism as the way to God," not hesitating to project a God consonant with human experience. Let us admit frankly that the only philosophical way to God open to man is to understand "a God fashioned wholly by human tools to serve human needs and conceptualized in a wholly human way." If someone is scandalized by such candor and protests that such a humanly created God could bear no relationship to the true God, he is obviously begging the question. He is simply assuming what he cannot test. "We do not know the true God."[9]

WAYS OF KNOWING

Someone may protest, however, that we do know God by analogy at least—as Thomas Aquinas was at pains to show. We know God as the cause of creatures; the very existence of a limited being is explained only by the infinite. We know God by supereminence; from any quality we discover on earth, we conclude to the Being who has this quality in an unlimited degree. The response here could be, of course, that to "know" God by any kind of analogy is still to be sure only of creatures. What we say concerning God remains conjecture and projection—no matter what polite words we use to disguise the process. Analogical knowledge has to be understood analogically—which is another way of admitting that we just do not know God.

But, someone can protest further, we do know God by faith. The response here is that faith is a leap and a commitment to the Ultimate without our experiencing the Ultimate as a fact. Any verbal content of faith is what we ourselves pour into the act of faith. "If faith puts us in communion with the absolute mystery we call God, there is a sense in which faith does not answer anything."[10]

Again one could protest, it's obvious that we know God from Scripture. After all, the Bible is the very word of the Lord. But the response here would have to be that if God is in any way the kind of spirit we say He is, then He can no more speak real human words than He has physical divine lips with which to say them. Words are human words even when God inspires them. The testaments Old and New are proclamations by people who pointed to Mystery as best they could: with figures of speech such as "salvation" and "redemption," "Lord" and "word of the Lord." The truth is that all "explicitly religious language (e.g., the language of the Scriptures or of the Christian mystics) is intrinsically symbolic and metaphorical 'limit-language'" about what we cannot sense as fact.[11]

Perhaps no one alive today has ever heard a sermon on the unknowability of God, yet such a sermon could be wholly respectable and in the ancient Christian tradition of negative or apophatic theology. Professionals (at least in their candid moments) and mystics seem sooner or later to arrive at less about God rather than more. For instance, Dupré, having sifted libraries in several languages, can remark:

> I see no alternative but to assume that God remains unspeakable after all has been said and that

revelation ultimately manifests the impenetrable darkness of the divine mystery.[12]

What we are looking at here is the inadequacy of classical theology. It became abstract and unrealistic, neglecting the subjective side of faith life. Preoccupied with being an official and approved system of ideas, it stressed content and objective statements.

Of course any theology will be inadequate when measured against what we claim to believe, but it's a matter of continually testing and purifying to evolve what would seem a less inadequate theology: an abiding problem with the theology of the Latin manuals was that it emerged from a defensive period of the Catholic Church. It was a standard and highly systematized body of propositions to be transmitted to seminarians throughout the world. With an eye on the enemies outside the citadel, it set undue store upon logical consistency and uniform wording. Classical theology elaborated the intellectual side of being Christian. But in the process faith came to look mainly like assent to propositions and ended by seeming easy because saying right words comes easy. Personal struggle was scarcely an issue; one had only to believe as the Church taught.

To an extent we have drawn a caricature here. But it seems clear that after the Reformation something vital was lost in official Catholic theology: the sense of depth and mystery. Vatican II was a massive step toward dismantling the citadel, but the consequences of the older formation remain. Rahner points out, for instance, that when faith is made highly verbal and objective, then it becomes easy for us to "talk of God as if we had already slapped him on the shoulder." Having neglected our "primitive experiences" of God in life, "our religious life is and remains really of a secondary character."[13] This verbal faith then is mostly a matter of the head, not of the person.

We may claim that we have outgrown such a rationalistic kind of faith. Yet we might also suspect that we cannot even recognize the thoroughness of our indoctrination. To see what may have happened to us even on the level of ideas, it can be useful to reflect on the following statements (admittedly lifted out of context). Which ones seem dangerous or heretical, and which seem soundly Christian?

> 1) Since we cannot know what God is but only what He is not, we cannot investigate how God exists but only how He is not.

> 2) This, then, is the best knowledge we can have about God in this life: that He is above every thought we can have about Him.

> 3) Whatever knowledge our intellect can have of God fails adequately to represent Him. And thus what God is always remains hidden from us.

> 4) Concerning God, we cannot understand what He is, but what He is not, and what is the relation of other things to Him.

> 5) Having arrived at the outer boundary of our knowledge, we know God as unknown. . . . That He is is known, but what He is remains unknown.

Each of the quotations is from Thomas Aquinas.[14] Despite his care with words and his many distinctions, he did not let logic obscure his sense of truth and mystery. Although the approaches differ, the Unknown God that Thomas points to is the Mystery Present of contemporary Catholic theology.

A Renewed Approach

It would be a book in itself to sketch out and defend the most helpful approach to our knowledge of God today.[15] But for our purposes here, we could say that a renewed approach to the God-problem could be diagrammed as four moments. This pedagogical analysis seems to agree with what philosophers of religion and theologians are saying today. But whether or not all this is academically proper, the important point is that it is useful to check this approach against our own experience.

1) *Intimations of Mystery*

When we put aside distraction and listen to our depths we may discover glimmerings of what is more than self, intimations of unlimit and beyondness. Perhaps by our schooling we consider as respectable knowledge only that which can be expressed in word or number. But our experience in hearing music, for example, reveals how a deeper awareness beyond words can be both elusive and real. Thus we may enjoy an evening with friends, feeling how marvelous if we could go on forever and ever. In this manner our primary religious experience will be intimations or hints of what beckons us dimly yet ever remains out of reach.

Rahner maintains that we grasp God in each of our acts of awareness, as the preconceptual horizon of knowledge, as the Whither of transcendence. This is actually to experience God, but as Mystery unthematized, before words. Other writers like to point to particular experiences where the intimations may be more vivid. Thus Gregory Baum points to depth experiences that are specifically "religious" (times of awe, of fear and terror) and experiences considered "secular" (feelings of friendship, or moral obligation, of truth, of compassion). These experiences we take as our response to some transcending presence.[16]

The term "peak experience" has been popularized by the psychologist Maslow. Turning from a study of sick people to those living life at its fullest (whether musicians, homemakers, athletes, business men), Maslow discerned that their highest moments of creativity or insight or performance all seemed to open up on the same ecstatic level described by mystics of East and West. Sexual experience, in like manner, will not differ fundamentally from work, aesthetic, or prayer experience, since "any male and any female" can "experience the transcendent and unitive, both in oneself and in the other."[17]

Any road can lead to such graced moments—joy or pain, work or leisure, good or evil. But perhaps some of the most bitter experiences in life can be the most transforming. A family loses its breadwinner through death by cancer, so that as never before the wife and children are driven to reaffirm life decisively. We may have an alcoholic friend who lives daily with a special awareness of what within himself is more than human. We hear how a friend is crushed in a car accident, and we are overwhelmed by the feeling of helplessness, realizing that we are easy targets for a death that no man can control.

Any such experience going beneath the surface reveals a dimension of ourselves that we can term "religious." We may transcend the ordinary when we feel wrenched for a friend beaten into a corner by medical bills. Whether by pain or by delight, we are pushed to the limits and feel certainly, if mutely, that there is a beyond. Whatever opens our depths to us we count as basically religious, even if there is no connection with church or institution. What is fundamentally religious in our experience is, in Tillich's phrase, what comes to us as our "ultimate concern."

But all this, one may object, is to make religious experience something ordinary and commonplace. How then can we tell religious experience from, for example, the satisfaction of a good dinner? One reply could be that there is no reason why they cannot be the same—so long as the afterglow of the meal opens up to some vista on life and living. Experience of our religious dimension, being aware of presence and unlimit, is actually available to anybody at any time. It is significant that both Jewish and Catholic ritual focus on food and drink. Table fellowship can be a human sharing that also reveals to us the divine. Sacramental moments may occur in church, but may just as well occur at home or at a restaurant or bar. Religious experience is not then restricted to any particular time or place, nor to any particular people. Nevertheless it is never commonplace, since as an experience of the unlimited it is our sensing of the extraordinary aspect of the ordinary.

2) Presence Intimated

Certain of our experiences particularly seem to point to something beyond our perceived limits. Thus when we decide to do the honest thing, even if nobody will catch us if we cheat, we may be aware of an elusive presiding spirit filling the universe. We love or are loved, and are led to embrace a boundlessness beyond human conception.

We apply the term "transcendence" to the elusive unlimited that measures the concrete limited we know before us. This unlimited or infinite arrives unnamed and outside of our control. Traditionally men have associated this ineffable beyond with the core of religion. "In transcendence therefore is found, in the form of the aloof and distant which rules unruled, the nameless being which is infinitely holy. This we call mystery, or rather, the *holy mystery*."[18]

We are aware of Mystery Present, but not as some thing we can handle or as some person we can exchange with. All we have to go on are hints that there is presence. These are experiences of the real, we are convinced, but they occur inarticulate. We attempt to image and verbalize them, but they flow like aesthetic experience, at levels deeper than ideas. Human experience is multi-dimensional.

Hence in its method contemporary theology is partly phenomenological. Its emphasis is not the logic of the Five Ways featured in classical theology. Instead it is reflection upon human experience. Contemporary theology is from man's side, anthropological. It proceeds on the pragmatic evidence that somehow mystery is found within ourselves. As Rahner suggests, man is "that which God becomes if he sets out to show himself in the region of the extra-divine." This means that "man is he who realises himself when he gives himself away into the incomprehensible mystery of God."[19]

But in using the term "God" we are of course ahead of our story. We want to concentrate on our experience of transcendence, putting aside any traditional titles. There is the danger that we have the word so much at our command that we can presume also to manipulate the reality it refers to. Whereas if we attend to our actual experience as we confront the unfathomable depth of our interior, rather than multiplying words, we tend to fall wondering and silent.

3) Assent and Commitment

The beyond impinges upon our awareness, but not as an inescapable datum. Especially if we hurry through life busy and distracted, we could miss the intimations. Even church work, theological discussion, and social action—and praying itself—can be a kind of busyness that shuts out depth experience. Yet once we sense the beyond of our depths, we have to take some sort of stand between a Yes or a No.

The intimations can accumulate into converging probabilities that make the leap of faith possible and reasonable. Hence even though we are not guided by factual knowing, our leap is not wholly blind. We do experience glimmerings. Faith is then a saying Yes to life as we find it, even in the face of sin and suffering. It is personal commitment to the ultimate within our experience. Obviously this can be a lifetime project, trying to say a whole-hearted Yes.

As an act of trust, as a movement from some particular good or grace to all the goodness and graciousness we feel must be, our faith is a Yes to what we can only hope in. This is fundamental faith in life. It need not arrive at church dogmas and creeds in order to be faith. It is a confidence in the universe, a trust that there is goodness, truth, justice beyond what we actually find in the world: greed, stupidity, falseness, oppression. Our "basic confidence and trust in existence," says Tracy, "*is* our fundamental faith, our basic authentic mode of being in the world."[20]

While thus far we have pictured faith as a leap over a chasm, from some hint in our experience to an existing ultimate, still in another sense faith is a leaning back and relaxing—a flowing along in the direction our very nature and experience carry us. We simply cease to resist, to run, to control—and finally say "Yes, let it be."

4) Expressing Faith

The leap of faith does not remain interior and unexpressed. As a human activity it includes exteriorization, as

word and symbol, as ritual and practice. We not only articulate our faith for ourselves, but we also communicate our
stance. We say of it whatever we can say.

In real life the individual's leap of faith is evoked within
a community that will have symbols to express it. The world
religions are the more or less institutionalized articulations
of the religious impulse. They preserve sacred writings, set
up shrines, establish bureaus. They tell stories and employ
myths to say what is of ultimate concern—whether life is
worth living, how to live, what can be beyond death. Communities called Christian profess to find their meaning best
illustrated and expressed in Jesus, especially in God's work
of transforming Him.

But then there are problems. Especially in the case of
traditional religion, the exterior expressions of faith are
ambiguous. Hymns and creeds can be vocalized as if the
entire group shares equally and fully. Group practice can
conceal individual differences and needs. Community religion is at its worst when it enforces its symbols upon the
young in such a way that a person may never connect with
his depth experience. In a community of adults thus indoc-
trinated since youth, there is the problem of inauthentic
religion, false conscience, verbal faith, and so on.

Contemporary theology can be a force for self-criticism
and personal renewal. It can encourage us to get in better
touch with ourselves, where we will find grace and revelation and salvation going on. It is significant that in his presidential address to a convention of the Catholic Theological
Society, Richard McBrien describes the mission of professional theologians in these terms:

> We are actually doing theology only when we are
> in the process of struggling to articulate, in a more

or less systematic manner, our presumed perception of the transcendent in our contemporary
experience and in our corporate histories. Theology is an orderly reflection on our experience of
God. Christian theology is an orderly reflection on
our experience of God as definitively disclosed in
Jesus Christ.[21]

To sum up, then, the best of what contemporary theology
seems to come to is this: a prophetic call back to our depths.
In and with our depths we are aware as a whole person when
we experience an unlimited dimension in living. At any time
and in any place we may be conscious of the endless aspect
of life, but certain occasions prove to be more revealing than
others. As we hurtle downhill on skis, for instance, we may
be alive as at no other moment, experiencing a boundlessness and timelessness. We feel convinced that we contact God
in some total, immediate, but unsensed manner. We do not
experience God as some outside thing, neither as some object
we can touch on earth nor as a king on a throne in outer
space. In an incarnational universe, God is in and with all
experience as the unfathomable dimension. Contemporary
theologians, both Protestant and Catholic, emphasize this
experiential foundation for theological reflection.

NOTES

1. For a representative Latin manual, see the fourth edition of Pietro Parente, *De Deo uno et trino* (Torino: Marietti, 1956).

2. Karl Rahner, "On the Theology of the Incarnation," *Theological Investigations*, vol. 4, trans. Kevin Smyth (Baltimore: Helicon Press, 1966), p. 116.

3. Bruce Vawter, *This Man Jesus: An Essay toward a New Testament Christology* (Garden City: Doubleday, 1973), p. 17.

4. Joseph A. Fitzmyer, "Belief in Jesus Today," Commonweal Papers: 5, *Commonweal* 101 (15 November 1974): 139.

5. Ibid., p. 140.

6. Ibid., p. 141.

7. Avery Dulles, *The Survival of Dogma* (Garden City: Doubleday, 1971), p. 146.

8. Ibid., p. 144.

9. Daniel Callahan, "Human Experience and God," in *American Philosophy and the Future: Essays for a New Generation*, ed. Michael Novak (New York: Scribner, 1968), p. 243-244.

10. Dulles, *Survival of Dogma*, p. 139.

11. David Tracy, "Religious Language as Limit-language," *Theology Digest* 22 (Winter 1974): 295.

12. Louis K. Dupré, *The Other Dimension: A Search for the Meaning of Religious Attitudes* (Garden City: Doubleday, 1972), p. 292.

13. Karl Rahner, *The Priesthood* (New York: Seabury, 1973), p. 8.

14. *Summa theologiae*, I, 3, *prooem. De veritate*, 2, 1, ad 9. *De veritate*, 2, 1, ad 9. *Contra gentes*, I, 30. *In librum Boetii de Trinitate expositio*, I, 2, ad 1.

15. See for example the essay by David Tracy, *Blessed Rage for*

Order: The New Pluralism in Theology (New York: Seabury Press, 1975).

16. Gregory Baum, *Faith and Doctrine: A Contemporary View* (Paramus: Newman Press, 1969), pp. 59-86.

17. Abraham H. Maslow, *Religions, Values, and Peak-experiences* (New York: Viking Press, 1964), p. 116.

18. Karl Rahner, "The Concept of Mystery in Catholic Theology," *Theological Investigations*, vol. 4, trans. Kevin Smyth (Baltimore: Helicon Press, 1966), p. 53.

19. Karl Rahner, "Anonymous Christians," *Theological Investigations*, vol. 6, trans. Karl-H. and Boniface Kruger (Baltimore: Helicon Press, 1969), p. 393.

20. David Tracy, *Blessed Rage for Order: The New Pluralism in Theology* (New York: Seabury Press, 1975), p. 134.

21. Richard P. McBrien, "Catholic Theology, 1974: Problems and Prospects," (Presidential Address) Proceedings of the Catholic Theological Society of America 29 (1974): 399.

3 The Central Message

WHAT IS the central message of contemporary theology? Among the personalist and existentialist writers at least, the major theme can be identified as Mystery Present. Mystery Present is not God seated on a throne above the clouds. Nor is He even the Interior Master of St. Augustine. Such spatial images could imply that God is located outside us or inside us, while we are left as observers. Whereas actually, as Baum reminds us, "there is no human standpoint from which God is simply man's over-against."[1] In other words, we can expect to evolve no final metaphors. We can only continue to wrestle with the articulation of our experience. We may feel certain that we ourselves are not Mystery Present, but we can suspect that all we are He is. This would mean that "to try to see God is like trying to look at your own eyes, for he is nearer to us than we are to ourselves."[2]

Mystery Present is the ubiquitous God of classical theology, so far as we emerge within Him and are immersed in Him, as in a field of force. But the classical Omnipresent is concluded to within a logical context, whereas contemporary theology insists on starting with awareness of glimmerings in our depths.

MYSTAGOGY

Contemporary theology approaches the Ultimate, therefore, from experience. Its program is pragmatic. To the
dismay of its critics, perhaps, contemporary Catholic theology stands on the side of mysticism.

Rahner has chosen a word for it: *mystagogy*. This is the
approach of a person who has been attentive to his depth
experiences, who then invites another to listen to his own
organism. This is the approach of the Christian in secular
society, who respects the interior revelation available to his
neighbors. This is the approach of the missionary who goes
not to benighted pagans but to people already in touch with
the divine. This is the approach, moreover, to the villain
of the textbooks, the atheist. Someone who has looked into
himself or herself can readily understand how, for instance,
a person rejecting the God of organized religion can still
be "aware of his own transcendental knowledge of God
through a kind of 'mystagogy.'"3

Mystagogy, furthermore, would seem the only workable
approach to young people, especially now to the world-weary
students of television. We hear predictions about younger
people abandoning not only the Church but also all faith.
But men like Rahner do not seem unduly worried, since "it
is not so easy to run past the infinite Mystery."4

Honesty and Mystery are the issue here. The earnest
searcher "may be far from the officially constituted Christianity; he may feel like an atheist, he may think fearfully
that he does not believe in God." But we accept each other
where we are, encouraging everyone to walk according to
his light. "Ally yourself with what is genuine, with the challenging, with what demands everything, with the courage to
accept the mystery within you."5

Mystagogy may strike older Catholics as something alien or even heretical. Such a reaction would indicate, as one factor, the success of rationalism in the Western churches. We have come to feel that we manage and control only what we have words for. We expect answers in clear-edged concepts. In the schools, indoctrination with right formulations has helped make faith in God look easy, because even children can be facile with words. As a consequence, "a great many Christians, even priests, often speak unwittingly of God as though he had appeared to them in human form."[6]

A remedy for this cheap faith of words is renewal through mystical experience—not the exotic mysticism described classically by William James—but the depth experience possessed by everyone. This is our fundamental religious experience, vaguely felt and not yet verbalized. Whatever we can say and do about God that will be real for us has to grow out of this personal experience. "All that man has then to say of this God can never be more than a pointer to this primitive experience of God."[7] To read the New Testament, then, is more like comparing notes than it is receiving what we do not have.

As a program, mystagogy is contemporary in its conscious interiority and subjectivity. It arrives as something new in the Catholic Church, where "objective faith" has been stressed officially for the past four centuries.

But mystagogy is also a return to the contemplative tradition found in the great religions. Jesus himself, presented to us as a Jew attentive to his depths, stands in this prayer tradition. "He is a true mystagogue," says Gray, "in that he leads others into the divine mystery of giving which, like the true mystic, he has first tasted himself."[8] So much, then, for the first conclusion, that contemporary Catholic theology fosters an awareness of God's presence within each person.

JESUS AS MEDIATOR

A second conclusion concerns the trinitarian status of Mystery Present. In re-examining religious life today we have to ask painful questions. Have we set up, for instance, an image of Jesus and called it God? Have Jesus practices got in the way of our relating to the Unknown?

Until recently, to take a case in point, parish practices were dominated by the image of Jesus. Thus, much energy went into First Fridays and services to the Sacred Heart. More significantly, Mass and Benediction were thought of as a kind of Jesus devotion. The Real Presence of Jesus was accepted as the purpose of the Eucharist, so that the consecration became the climax of the Mass, announced by the ringing of bells. The moment of elevation of the species was prolonged into Benediction, when the visible Jesus was exhibited in a monstrance placed upon the altar throne. The throne, and the tabernacle beneath it, were the focus of the parish church.

Now that practice has been reshaped in the light of history and theory, churches today feature a plain table. The Eucharist is fundamentally the thanksgiving prayer to God. Jesus can be understood to have a priestly role in the Mass, but "God is the only central point."[9] The sacraments are in the name of Jesus, but they are not Jesus devotions.

Taking its cue from the New Testament, contemporary theology understands God as the ultimate and Jesus as His herald and mediator. This subordinate relationship informs every book of the New Testament, no matter how human Jesus is taken to be, or how divine and pre-existent. "Father" and "Son" is the basic set of correlative terms to indicate priority in mission and function. The Father of course is the Unoriginate, *ho theos* or God. "When the New Testament

thinks of God, it is the concrete, individual, uninterchange-
able Person who comes into its mind, who is in fact the
Father."[10]

Jesus came in obedience to preach the kingdom. "The
kingdom of God," in a word, "means an immediate relationship to the Father."[11] Jesus came to reveal the wonder of
His Father's presence, most especially in transformation at
death. The early communities remembered Jesus as being
most careful not to assume honor for Himself. All His deeds
and words say, in effect, "Not me, friends, but my Father."

Thus Jesus invited disciples to follow; to imitate Christ
is to orient self and community to God. He taught friends
how to pray; they prayed not to Him but to "Our Father."
Jesus Himself prayed to *Abba*, Father. This lifelong rev-
erence to God, ending in agony on Calvary, leads Moran to
observe: "the paradox of a religion centered on Jesus Christ
is that it might not speak much about Jesus Christ."[12] "Jesus
Christ," Sloyan concludes, "is not central to our faith and
prayer; God alone is that."[13] Mystery Present and not Jesus
is the primary object of Christian worship and life.

Devotees of Mystery

A third conclusion is that God the Unknown is the very
point of the Christian Church. And this is radically what it
means to be a Roman Catholic: to be a devotee of Mystery.
For "Christian Faith says nothing more than that we have
been called into the immediacy of the mystery of God himself and that this mystery gives itself to us in unspeakable
nearness."[14] The core of Christianity, Rahner maintains,
is the Holy Unknown. "This is the real content of Christianity: the ineffability of the absolute mystery which be-

stows itself in forgiveness and in drawing us into its own divine nature."[15]

> This, then, is how we should sum up Christianity as a whole: Christianity is the assent on the part of the whole community (Church) formulated and held explicitly by that community to the absolute mystery which exercises an inescapable power in and over our existence, and which we call God. It is our assent to that mystery as pardoning us and admitting us to a share in its own divinity, it is that mystery as imparting itself to us in a history shaped by man's own free decisions as an intelligent being; and this self-bestowal of God in Jesus Christ manifests itself as finally and irrevocably victorious in history.[16]

Here is the call to a profound and naked faith. It is not a summons to the faith of our fathers, if such a faith means to remain content with a set of comfortable symbols beyond which we do not search. Tillich urges us to worship the God beyond God—the Reality beyond any concept or metaphor we can form. This shattering of communal and national and cultural images is the obligation of authentic believers. Genuine faith cannot rest in anything man-made but must ever stretch toward the real Unreachable.

We are caught in a dilemma, then. On the one hand religion has to cherish its heritage of familiar images, hymns, creeds, doctrines, practices, edifices, and so on. To abandon these is to lose identity and continuity. On the other hand, to repose in such thematizations sanctified by history can be to idol-ize them. It is idolatry because it "amounts to identifying with God ourselves and the world which we ourselves want to uphold and defend."[17]

There are many kinds of idols that block relationship with Mystery Present. There is, for instance, "the child's sweet, kind God," and "the God taken for granted by so-called 'good christians,' who behave as if they could not understand the atheists' anxiety and uncertainty." There are also the various illusions of self-satisfied Christian piety: "if we think that everything ought to make sense . . . if we think that things ought to go well for us," or "if we think that God must be at our disposal as long as and because we serve him."[18]

Since Christianity "aims at bringing man into contact with God as the ineffable mystery" beyond the reach of man, "Christianity constitutes a radical denial of all such idols." The Christian God is a Mystery God, not pinned down by words or logic, not boxed in by human knowing or planning, in no way embraced by creeds or prayers or sacrifices. "Christianity recognizes that man knows God only when he is reduced to silence and adoration by the experience of this mystery."[19]

PASTORAL ORIENTATION

Now a fourth conclusion is this: Contemporary theology is pastorally oriented. The speculation and scholarship is less for system-building than for living. We can expect to experience the true God only when we get in touch with ourselves. Whether this is done in solitude or in conversation with others, the issue seems to be that we remain open to whatever experience brings. Each person has to proceed as he feels drawn by the Spirit. As Rahner notes, in spite of all our talk about God, specialists in theology and prayer life have developed no helpful method. In one passage, however, he ventures advice like this:

Be still for once. Don't try to think of so many
complex and varied things. Give these deeper
realities of the spirit a chance now to rise to the
surface: silence, fear, the ineffable longing for
truth, for love, for fellowship, for God. Face lone-
liness, fear, imminent death! Allow such ultimate,
basic human experiences to come first. Don't go
talking about them, making up theories about
them, but simply endure these basic experiences.
Then in fact something like a primitive awareness
of God can emerge.[20]

Valuable testimony on this matter is available from
people who have spent a life at religion in both East and
West. Alan Watts is convinced that "if God is real, he need
not be sought in any particular direction or conceived in
any special way." To be ready for what comes, "it is only
necessary to stop dreaming and open the eyes."[21] William
Johnston, in his turn, observes that there is no one Christian mysticism, and "no established technique," and "no
clear-cut path." He thinks that "to the end, Christian mysticism will remain something of a journey without maps."[22]

OBJECTIONS TO MYSTAGOGY

Now all this may be well and good, one may say, but there
are some objections. To begin with an obvious one, if this
theme of Mystery Present is so central in contemporary
theology, then why do we hear so little about it in school and
church? One response could be that Christianity itself "can
often be so very empty" and can thus "be used as a means of
escape before the mystery instead of openly facing up to it."[23]
Being a loyal parishioner, for instance, is no guarantee of being

genuinely religious. Our "primitive, nameless and theme-less experience" can be "buried by our daily routine" and "even through our theological, ascetic and pious chatter."[24]

This is not a malaise only in the Catholic Church, of course. All "modern Church religion is little concerned with giving any consciousness of union with God." No church of the West is a mystical religion in Watt's view; therefore none is "fully and essentially religion."[25] What happens then, as recent history shows, is that a "Christianity which is not basically mystical must become either a political ide-ology or a mindless fundamentalism."[26]

Having lost the sense of mystery after the Reformation, official Catholic theology is only beginning to rediscover it. But actual church reform so far seems to rely on an older model of revelation: things will get back to normal once we finish translating the ancient words into contemporary terms—as if it were largely a question of packaging and salesmanship.

Charismatic movements seem to be one indication that some people, anyhow, need a warm medium with which to express their depth experience. With novenas and parish devotions taken away, there is only the Sunday service, which for many does not seem to convey mystery or to touch the heart. "Obviously, if Christian groups cannot or will not provide mystical religion, the work will be . . . done by Hindus, Buddhists, Sufis, unaffiliated gurus, and growth centers."[27]

Rahner insists that "one's direct personal relationship with God . . . constitutes the immutable essence of Chris-tian living."[28] Renewal is not simply a matter of brighter textbooks, more meetings, or Mass in English with guitars. The first principle will have to be: respect for depth experience. What program of catechetics and preaching could help us appreciate our depth experience? What liturgy can be devised to express better our depth experience?

Then there is a second possible objection, that devotion to Mystery appears to be elitist. It would be a luxury limited to those with leisure and with a taste for the hermit's life.

By way of response, it can be agreed that such devotion would be for a chosen few if it were a question of long hours and of visions. But there is an authentic devotion to Mystery that is simply a respect for the religious dimension of our daily life. "Mystical experience," says Johnston, "is not something exotic but a deepened form of an ordinary human experience."[29] Attention to our depths cannot be something left to monks. Response to our depth experience entails a degree of contemplative prayer possible to anyone serious about life.

There is the real problem, however, that we have no tradition of ordinary lay mysticism. We have heard about fantastic visions of the saints, and we are emerging from an era where public recitation of prayers was common (the rosary, for example). But between recited formulas and classical mysticism, we really have no model of prayer to fall back on. However, at weekend encounters and retreats— and in mind control classes—some people can experiment with prayer forms that explore depth experiences.

Related to the charge of elitism is a third objection, that devotion to Mystery Present is individualistic. This objection issues from the fact that love for God *is* strongly individual, like the act of dying. There comes a point where no one else may go further with you. So that there is simply no alternative to the deeply private risk that each one takes in affirming Mystery. Each of us has to let go of himself, to be willing to fall millions of miles into the void—or into the fullness. It remains a private vocation—which is not at all to imply that one must be a professional contemplative.

Devotion to Mystery Present is going to be individualistic only if it stops with the individual, as was illustrated in the thrust of recent popular piety. It was oriented toward Jesus-and-me. Heaven was preached as individual salvation—after death. The sacred was sharply distinct from the secular, with church being the refuge of the sacred. Religion was to provide maximum comfort and security, with a minimum of involvement in social and political affairs. American churches were to certify the American way of life. But today, clearly, we have come to ask hard questions about the implications of such privatistic religion.

Now while genuine devotion to Mystery Present has its private aspect, it is also communal. Love of God is what community religion is all about. Group tradition enables each member better to locate, interpret, and celebrate his depth experiences. In community ritual, depth experience finds expression, even prolongation and intensification. Graced moments, however, are not restricted to the traditional seven sacraments. All of life, in fact, is sacramental and can mediate our awareness of Mystery. So long as we are open to them, graced moments can break in on us at work or play, alone or with others.

"The Good News," Baum writes, "is that God is present to human life."[30] Our response to Mystery Present, then, is a reaching out to all of the human race. We reach out, of course, to the like-minded people of our Spirit-filled church community, where we can explicitly proclaim the good news and celebrate it. But we reach out as well to all other people in a Spirit-filled world, where the church community signifies union with Mystery and the formation of brotherhood that constitutes the kingdom of God.

Hence devotion to Mystery Present is not only each one's private prayer in his chamber, to his Father in secret. Such devotion also follows the flow of love energy in the universe (1 John 4:10-11): because Mystery has first loved us, we share the gift-love with each other. Devotees of Mystery reach out in concern and care. Solitary adoration in silence and concrete social action need not exclude each other. Devotees of Mystery Present would especially be the people who remove structures that oppress the powerless.[31]

To conclude, what contemporary personalist theology is emphasizing has been pointed at through the centuries, even if in recent times it was obscured. Francis Thompson said it dramatically in his stunning image of the Hound of Heaven: our completion comes when we quit trying to be in control, when we let ourselves be embraced and loved without limit. We are pursued by the Father whom no man knows (John 1:18 and 6:46; 1 John 4:12 and 20). He looks eagerly for our return as Prodigal Sons and Daughters. He is the Incomprehensible who dwells as Mystery Present, having pitched His tent among us. In fact, Mystery Present indwells, as within a temple, as within each individual. Mystery is God and God the Father. In stressing this elementary lesson, contemporary theology returns to the fundamental truth that contains any others. All theology can be held in the palm of the hand: there is one and only one truth—Mystery Present.

NOTES

1. Gregory Baum, *Man Becoming: God in Secular Language* (New York: Herder and Herder, 1970), p. 170.

2. Alan Watts, *Behold the Spirit: A Study in the Necessity of Mystical Religion* (New York: Vintage Books, 1971), p. 17.

3. Karl Rahner, "Atheism and Implicit Christianity," *Theological Investigations*, vol. 9, trans. Graham Harrison (New York: Herder and Herder, 1972), p. 159.

4. Karl Rahner, "Thoughts on the Possibility of Belief Today," *Theological Investigations*, vol. 5, trans. Karl-H. Kruger (Baltimore: Helicon Press, 1966), p. 21.

5. Ibid., p. 21.

6. Karl Rahner, *Do You Believe in God?*, trans. Richard Strachan (New York: Newman Press, 1969), p. 105.

7. Karl Rahner, *The Priesthood*, trans. Edward Quinn (New York: Herder and Herder, 1973), p. 9.

8. Donald P. Gray, "The Incarnation: God's Giving and Man's Receiving," *Horizons* 1 (Fall 1974): 13.

9. Karl Rahner, *The Christian Commitment: Essays in Pastoral Theology*, trans. Cecily Hastings (New York: Sheed and Ward, 1963), p. 140.

10. Karl Rahner, "Theos in the New Testament," *Theological Investigations*, vol. 1, trans. Cornelius Ernst (Baltimore: Helicon Press, 1961), p. 146.

11. Piet Schoonenberg, *The Christ: A Study of the God-Man Relationship in the Whole of Creation and in Jesus Christ*, trans. Della Couling (New York: Herder and Herder, 1971), p. 102.

12. Gabriel Moran, *The Present Revelation: The Search for Religious Foundations* (New York: Herder and Herder, 1972), p. 267.

13. Gerard S. Sloyan, "Some Implications of Theology for Religious Education," *PACE* 3 (1972): Trends—Perspectives—D, p. 1.

14. Rahner, "Thoughts on the Possibility of Belief Today," p. 21.

15. Karl Rahner, "Intellectual Honesty and Christian Faith," *Theological Investigations*, vol. 7, trans. David Bourke (London: Darton, Longman and Todd, 1971), p. 63.

16. Ibid., p. 60.

17. Rahner, *The Priesthood*, p. 11.

18. Ibid., pp. 11-12.

19. Rahner, "Intellectual Honesty and Christian Faith," p. 61.

20. Rahner, *The Priesthood*, pp. 7-8.

21. Watts, *Behold the Spirit*, pp. xxiii-xxiv.

22. William Johnston, *The Still Point* (New York: Fordham University Press, 1970), p. 25.

23. Rahner, "Thoughts on the Possibility of Belief Today," p.8.

24. Rahner, *The Priesthood*, p. 9.

25. Watts, *Behold the Spirit*, p. 5.

26. Ibid., p. xiii.

27. Ibid., p. xxi.

28. Karl Rahner, "Christian Living Formerly and Today," *Theological Investigations*, vol. 7, trans. David Bourke (London: Darton, Longman and Todd, 1971), p. 11.

29. Johnston, *The Still Point*, p. 34.

30. Baum, *Man Becoming*, p. 35.

31. On the issue of integrating the private, mystical side of life with the public, prophetic side, see Matthew Fox, *On Becoming a Musical, Mystical Bear: Spirituality American Style* (New York: Paulist Press, 1976), pp. 77-116.

4 The Difference Jesus Makes

WHAT DIFFERENCE does Jesus make?

In classical theology Jesus is Redeemer of course, and from Redemption emanates the rest of the Christian vision. There was creation, then Adam and his original sin—from this followed the Incarnation and a particular kind of Church with its dogmatic and sacramental systems. The plan of salvation hinged on Adam; the Incarnation occurred in view of Redemption. Jesus came as an activist mediator. In scholastic terms, he is somehow the efficient cause of our salvation.

But now we have to reevaluate this traditional picture. Educated people today assume an evolutionary origin for man, so that the sudden appearance of a perfect human couple in a Persian garden seems out of the question. Adam as a historical person finds no defenders, either, among contemporary Scripture experts, nor does original sin. Thus the whole structure of classical Redemption crashes down.

But once we abandon the original sin framework of Western tradition (including the hurried baptism of babies), what is left to say about the Christian faith we were brought up with? If Jesus is not to be the sweating, bleeding, anguished victim appeasing the angry Father, what other difference can he make?

Posed in this way, the question expresses the confusion

and dismay of older Catholics. Besides, this is a rational-istic sort of question, expecting a hard-edged answer.

ORIGINAL SIN

To begin with, let's see why contemporary writers no longer accept the original sin version of Redemption. This rejection of centuries of reflection is a significant shift. On the personal level, for people today caught in a transition period, the shift can mean pain since it alters the picture of salvation most of us were brought up on and which is more or less embedded in our nervous system.

It may be helpful to remind ourselves that no theological explanation can be adequate to the reality it points to. As man-made efforts to understand what we cannot know as verifiable facts, all theologies will be insufficient, incomplete, inconsistent, and heavily conditioned by the times. We should not be surprised, then, to find that the classical theories of atonement include components that never were satisfactorily reconciled. In general, we could say that theologies of the West (both Catholic and Protestant) have built on original sin as immediate motive for Redemption and have therefore put the burden on Adam. But from several directions the presuppositions of classical theology are challenged.

First, science will not allow us to talk about Adam and Eve as historical persons. From what archeologists like Richard Leakey find by excavating sites of early and pre-human activities, the human race could not have started with its Golden Age—neither with men at their best nor with the whole race issuing from a single couple. The earliest hominids may have existed as much as fourteen million years ago.

The Genesis story about Adam can scarcely be a chronicle of historical events.

Second, there are internal difficulties with the original-sin approach. How, for example, can a state of sin be transmitted by heredity? How could we attribute a state of sin to an infant? These are samples of problems insoluble in classical theology.

Third, among the internal difficulties are certain classical assumptions. The original sin approach assumes that in going to death out of obedience to God, Jesus was putting aright an upset order (according to Anselm's view at least). Yet why anybody at all had thus to go through pain and death was left vague and impersonal. When it was a matter of beasts, for example, it would be stated that an angry God was appeased by bloody sacrifice. But no one, of course, ever dared to say out loud that an angry Father was appeased by the death of His Son.

Nevertheless, in the preaching tradition anyhow, it was well understood that Jesus was sacrificed as the Lamb of God. After all, there are New Testament texts to prove that our salvation was achieved by the blood of Christ. An almost cannibal God, then, stood behind the elaborate Redemption system. Today we find this a repulsive presupposition. We realize that evil is a mystery and that there may be something deeply true about a need for Jesus to have died a mangled death. Still, we can theologize only on the premise that there is intelligence and order in the universe, and that the compassionate aspirations we find in ourselves existed as well in the early Christians.

Another troubling assumption behind the original sin story is this: would such an earth-shaking event as the coming of Jesus be a last-minute decision? Did he come only because Adam failed a test?

Fourth, the theory of original sin Redemption did not drop down from heaven; rather, it has a human history. Augustine in particular developed reasons to defend the practice of infant baptism. His synthesis, repeated by the councils of Carthage (in 418) and of Orange (in 529), was incorporated into the decrees of Trent (1546): we inherit sin by descent from Adam, and this sin must be removed by Christ through baptism. In the West this remained a fundamental belief, unquestioned for centuries.

The legal or juridical aspect of Redemption comes to us largely from another saint, Anselm of Canterbury. Because sin upsets the harmony of justice in the universe, this harmony must be restored by atonement. Jesus came as volunteer with infinite power to atone for Adam's offense against the infinite Lord. This version of Redemption, Vawter notes, seems "rather modern, libertarian, and high-principled," but it has "little or nothing to do with the biblical categories it purported to explain."[1]

A fifth challenge to original sin Redemption arises from a new awareness of hermeneutics or literary interpretation. Scripture experts and students of history realize that every document from the past has to be interpreted against its original context. Until recently, for instance, the Council of Trent was understood to have made monogenism (the human race originating from a single pair) an article of belief. A re-reading of the council decrees, however, would show that there is not "in Trent any direct reason for making monogenism a doctrine of faith."[2]

A sixth and most sharp challenge comes from Scripture experts. Classical Redemption theory depended on two biblical foundations: Genesis on Adam, and Romans 5:12 on Christ as the new Adam. Scholars today, though, explain how both passages have been misinterpreted, so that there is no way to prove that original sin is in the Bible—neither in these two places nor anywhere else.

The story about Adam and his fall had been accepted as historical fact for centuries because the Bible was taken literally as reporting. With the revival of ancient languages and literatures, it became clear that the Adam story was not history but etiology, that is, a reflection on the sinful condition of man by assigning a supposed cause for it. In Genesis, actually, the term "Adam" means a clod of earth. As for Romans 5:12, Augustine had thought that here his position was explicitly expressed in revelation: that *in Adam* all men had sinned. His view of original sin became the official doctrine of the West for fifteen hundred years.

But Erasmus first, and then Lyonnet recently, have shown that the Latin translation Augustine used was faulty, not corresponding to Paul's original Greek, where the important connective was *eph ho*, meaning "because" or "accordingly." Instead of talking about *Adam in whom* all have sinned (thus inherited sin, with one man responsible for that), Paul talked about death to all *because all* have committed personal sins. Based on the original Greek, translations today read like this one: "Therefore as sin came into the world through one man and death through sin, and so death spread to all men because all men sinned."[3]

It is evident that Augustine was misled, since there is "no teaching of original sin here."[4] Romans 5:12 is a literary device to highlight Christ's mission. It is not a statement that can support the weight of Western classical theology. Nor is original sin mentioned elsewhere in the Bible. "The idea that Adam's descendants are automatically sinners because of the sin of their ancestor, and that they are already sinners when they enter the world, is foreign to Holy Scripture."[5]

That the story about original sin could flourish as it did might be explained apart from its supposed foundation in the Bible. For it does effectively symbolize our daily experience of sin—not only personal sin but also sinful structures all around us. So as to prevent confusion, however, it is an image that we could put a moratorium on.

But, you might object, even if we dispense with original sin as a basic motivation in theology, that still leaves Christ as Redeemer of our personal sins. Let original sin be a distinct component in classical theory that would not be only dispensable but, as we now see, not biblical. Theology can keep unaltered its major image of Jesus. After all, we are explicitly told by Paul in several passages how "we have redemption through His blood."[6]

REDEMPTION

What we have to take up next, then, is the very notion of *redemption*. It is difficult to deal with classical Redemption because the term has come to mean for us the plain set of facts about salvation. In the New Testament, by contrast, it is used unsystematically to refer to God's work achieved in Jesus. It appears along with other reconciliation metaphors such as atonement, sacrifice, expiation, blood of Christ. It has no global or technical meaning. Its use in the New Testament is in line with the Jewish family tradition of helping out your own. Actually in the Old Testament it is a legal term, where to redeem is to liberate by ransoming a kinsman from indentured slavery.

Now although "redemption is not one of the major basic ideas of primitive Christianity," yet "by a paradox, the word has become a technical term in theology and popular language."[7] What initially was a minor metaphor gave color and shape to theology in the West.

It is a curious process indeed, notes Vawter, when a literary device becomes a kind of literal report. The New Testament proclaims God's work "in metaphor." But "succeeding generations tend to reify the poetry of their fathers, betraying thereby the demise of imagination and ushering in all manner of confusion"[8] The whole notion of atonement or redemption shifted when certain biblical words were, so to speak, lifted out of context, emptied of the original meaning, then refilled with "pagan" content stressing appeasement of a vengeful God.

Something like this process went on with another metaphor, "blood of Christ." Today we may find it repulsive, as if it had ghoulish overtones. In the New Testament context it connotes joyful reconciliation, since the image corresponds to the theory and practice of Hebrew religious expiation rituals. "These rites clearly suggest that the victim and its blood were not intended to be substitutions for the sinner," as if the animal victim got the punishment that the sinner deserved. "Rather the life-blood of the victim was considered to have the power of purifying the altar," the place where God was present to man. "With the pouring of the life-blood was removed all that impeded the flow of God's goodness to man."[9] To the early Jewish Christians the "blood of Christ" would have proclaimed the part Jesus played in clearing man's way to the Father. For our day we are invited to find our own idioms to say the same good news.

Now why bother to survey the history of technical matters like this? In order to see better why theology today is on solid ground when it puts aside the mythology and the emphasis of classical Redemption. This is not to say that an insight is worthy only when it comes from the Bible. Rather, we are seeing that when a theological system appears to be from the early Church but actually is not, then we can more freely deal with it in itself, assessing its distortions and limitations.

GOD THE REDEEMER

Perhaps the most critical distortion of classical Redemption was not that it relied on a mythology, nor even that it made a system out of a mere metaphor, but that it "ignored the terms of the biblical metaphor, according to which God was the one who *performed* rather than accepted the *apolytrosis* [redemption] in Christ Jesus."[10]

If we have to ask the question starkly, then it would be: Who really redeems—Jesus? or God? The New Testament answer would definitely be God.

Yet the classical answer, at least as transmitted by the preaching tradition, would seem to be Jesus. Sermons, Lenten lectures, prayers at the Stations of the Cross—all stressed the key role of the suffering Jesus. An implication drawn from the bleeding and agony was the gratitude we owe Jesus for taking on his shoulders the penalty of our sins. The focus was on Jesus.

There is a distinctively different emphasis in what may be one of the most ancient sermons of the early Church. As remembered in Acts, Peter understood the issue to be not Calvary but Easter, while the key figure was the Father.

> Men of Israel, hear these words: Jesus of Nazareth, a man attested to you by God with mighty works and wonders and signs which God did

through him in your midst, as you yourselves know—this Jesus . . . you crucified. . . . But God raised him up. . . .

This Jesus God raised up, and of that we are all witnesses. Being therefore exalted at the right hand of God, and having received from the Father the promise of the Holy Spirit, he has poured out this which you see and hear.[11]

The implication is that we are to glorify the Unknown Father, who gives us a lively hope based on what He did in Jesus. According to the tradition represented by this sermon, faith terminates in Mystery Present.

Theology today, then, returns to the original orientation of the Redemption metaphor. "The author of redemption is the Father," says Schokel. "Christ is never called redeemer but only mediator or executor." Preachers and teachers today should "insist on the role of the Father as a protagonist of the redemption." It is justified, however, to present Jesus as "realizer of this work."[12] Christian faith "is essentially an Easter-faith." It is a response to Jesus, but primarily "a response made to God manifest in Jesus Christ."[13] It is "belief in an *act* of God who *raised* Jesus from the dead."[14]

Redemption could well be another biblical term to put aside, lest we compound the confusion. What has to be proclaimed is not the term itself but the truth it points to: Mystery is present, even when we wander off. It is not God who turns away or is absent but ourselves. Mystery Present waits, as the Father watching for the return of the Prodigal. Hence our experience of guilt and of reconciliation in the presence of Mystery could be expressed in atonement images. Such images, new or ancient, are not about objectively tested facts but about our religious experience.

As we have seen here, therefore, current theology is doing three things concerning the classical Redemption. First, it rejects the original sin mythology. Second, it relativizes "redemption," locating it as originally another biblical metaphor to denote reconciliation. Lastly, it restores to Mystery Present the role of redeeming and reconciling.

JESUS EXEMPLAR

Yet once we put "Redemption" into perspective, then we are still left with the big question: What difference does Jesus make now—if any?

To characterize the best of what we might find in theology today, we could say (to use a scholastic category again) that Jesus is exemplary cause of salvation. That is, in him we find illumination and inspiration. By seeing what Mystery has done in him, we are drawn in hope to affirm the best we experience in ourselves. As exemplar, Jesus shines through history as the Risen, our Brother, the First Fruits of the human race. In him we see what it means to be human, what we are capable of.

As example to us, Jesus is no mere teacher of morality. It is important, of course, that we be sensitive to what he said and did about being good and knowing what is right. But the real point of His life is that he said Yes to the initiatives of Mystery Present. What God has revealed is not the Bible but, primarily, what Jesus allowed to be done in him.

> The example that Christ gives is not that human beings with human power can achieve redemption but that the same divine power that glorified Christ is available to every other human being and can achieve a similar glorification. Christ is an ex-

emplar, not merely by what he did, but by what he allowed God to do to him. We are called to surrender ourselves to the action of the Trinity as Christ surrendered himself.[15]

To have Jesus count, then, we do not need to make him into a doer, a sweating, panting producer of graces. He counts by the really vital way of illuminating, radiating, expanding our consciousness. For us Christians, "Jesus lights up what is taking place now" in our lives and in the lives of all men. It is true that we can be more or less aware of this without Christ. But with Jesus as example, our explicit consciousness of him can make "a significant, indeed decisive, difference."[16] Some people, like St. Paul, become visibly transformed by their awareness of Jesus.

But, someone might object, this is to tear the heart out of Christianity — to say that Jesus saves us by radiating mental signals or whatever. That would take the reality out of Calvary.

We are back where we started from, at the core issue. Apparently it all depends on our presuppositions and assumptions. If we take work and production as the norm of what is worthwhile, then our model is the bulldozer. We want a Redeemer and Savior who pushes and pulls to save us. That kind of savior is demanded by a religious vision of salvation in which Jesus, for example, has to fill up a big reservoir with the graces he earns in proportion to his suffering. Or if we see salvation in terms of changes in things, then we want a savior who will produce magical results. A model for this would be the alteration that baptism was supposed to make in the souls of babies.

But if the universe is not a warehouse cluttered with things, but in some way a unitary experience, then we may be spirits (lumpy spirits, but spirits nonetheless), and spirits who are "saved" by saying Yes to the Mystery we are immersed in. In that case, what we need most is not a physical push, nor a magical whammy, but just plain enspiriting: awareness, encouragement, consciousness-raising. "Expanded consciousness is rightly prized in contemporary life as one of the most crucial factors in the process of humanization."[17] Consciousness is what we live by.

The Gospel tells the good news that raises our consciousness. The Church, especially as a community that remembers, is "the community of raised consciousness."[18] Even "the power of sacraments and consequently the purpose of their existence is to be understood in terms of a quality of consciousness whose facilitation and development is their fundamental function."[19]

To say that Jesus came as our example is to say the best we know. In him we can understand who we are and what we also can be. This is the encouraging, the enspiriting difference that Jesus can make, to a distracted and weary world. Life can be worth living.

MAN AND THEREFORE GOD

Now why, one could ask, was nothing said above about Jesus as God? The answer would be that his divinity was simply not the issue. Whatever was said above will stand by itself, no matter whether we follow the high Christology of Alexandria or the low one of Antioch, or the explicit versus the implicit Christology identified by Brown.[20]

One reason why divinity would not seem to be an issue, to start with, is that apparently everything is somehow divine. Creation would mean that if God extrudes himself (so to speak) into our time and space, then nothing escapes divinity. God is all that we are, but while we are a concretization of the divine, we are not all that God is. (We should not let anyone scare us with the label "pantheist.") "Man is accordingly in the most basic definition that which God becomes if he sets out to show himself in the region of the extra-divine."[21]

Within this context, the problem about the "nature" of Jesus now shifts: if somehow everything is divine, if really "man is the potential brother of Christ" so that he is truly the spokesman for the group He actually belongs to[22] — then is Jesus unique, and if so how? The distinguishing trait now could be located in one's Yes. We free creatures, human beings, are already divine stuff, but we are also aware that we are expected to accept and to complete the process by saying Yes to joy and pain, to life and to death. Jesus would be unique because his Yes was most total. "The claim that Jesus is the (most) unique revelation of God would mean that his receptivity for divine communion was the greatest known to men."[23]

In any event, New Testament studies seem to make it clear that Jesus was genuinely human. "At whatever cost in terms of other cherished beliefs, the reality and normality of Jesus' manhood must be maintained." It is true that early in the Church there developed the suggestion of a pre-existing heavenly being who came down to earth to be called Jesus; this notion was one way to understand the divinity of Jesus, but from the start it also tended to obscure the humanity of Jesus. If we were forced to choose "between the pre-existence and a fully authentic human life," we should decide for the latter, since "the humanity is both more sure and more important than the pre-existence."[24]

This insistence on Jesus' humanness takes nothing away from his divinity, no matter how that would be understood.

But this emphasis does rectify the lopsidedness of a docetic tradition appearing in every age, which sees Jesus as a God who wore a human mask. Once in a while the mask slipped, as at the transfiguration, when the real Jesus shone through to reveal the God of power who commands the wind and the waves. This is the Jesus turned into an icon, effectively "deprived of all human content," playing a role as would an actor who memorized a script.[25] Here likely is the Jesus that adult Catholics today learned about in school and church.

But there is a purification of Jesus images going on today. Actually adults of every Christian church may have some reexamination to go through, as a kind of therapy. The Scripture experts especially promote what they see are correctives and norms. All this is the wrestling that has to go on in every age. "The Church must regard the Mysterium Christi as a reality which is continually to be thought through afresh."[26] The creed of Chalcedon, for instance, may have settled bitter controversy for an earlier era, but it may not be the kind of answer we need for our time.

Despite the varieties of stances on Jesus that have come down through history (more or less legitimate developments of New Testament traditions), we have to return to sources to see for ourselves what the initial reactions to Jesus were. Each person has to read and meditate, as Sister Mary Finn reminds us, so that we can write our own gospel.

> Each of us needs to go to Cana and Bethany and Jerusalem. We need to walk a long time with Him so that we can "write" the Gospel of Jesus according to who we are. There really is the Good News according to yourself. Matthew, Luke, John and Mark "wrote the Gospels," but so does every person who has seen Him.[27]

NOTES

1. Bruce Vawter, *This Man Jesus: An Essay toward a New Testament Christology* (Garden City: Doubleday, 1973), p. 75.

2. Piet Schoonenberg, *Man and Sin: A Theological View*, trans. Joseph Donceel (University of Notre Dame Press, 1965), p. 175.

3. *The New Testament of Our Lord and Savior Jesus Christ*, Revised Standard Version/Catholic Edition (Collegeville: Liturgical Press, 1965), Romans 5:12.

4. Herbert Haag, *Is Original Sin in Scripture?*, trans. Dorothy Thompson (New York: Sheed and Ward, 1969), p. 100.

5. Ibid., p. 106.

6. Ephesians 1:7.

7. John L. McKenzie, "Redemption," *Dictionary of the Bible* (Milwaukee: Bruce, 1965), p. 725.

8. Vawter, *This Man Jesus*, p. 75.

9. "Atonement," *The New World Dictionary-Concordance to the New American Bible* (New York: World Publishing, 1970), p. 44.

10. Vawter, *This Man Jesus*, p. 75.

11. Acts 2:22-24, 32-33.

12. Luis Alonso Schokel, "Why Christ Is Called Our Redeemer," *Theology Digest* 20 (Spring 1972): 56.

13. Joseph A. Fitzmyer, "Belief in Jesus Today," Commonweal Papers: 5, *Commonweal* 101 (November 15, 1974): 141.

14. Vawter, *This Man Jesus*, p. 45.

15. Seely Beggiani, "The Meaning of Christ's Redemption," *American Ecclesiastical Review* 166 (December 1972): 704-705.

16. Donald P. Gray, "The Place of Jesus in *Man's Becoming*," *The Ecumenist* 10 (March-April 1972): 43.

17. Donald P. Gray, "Sacramental Consciousness-Raising," *Worship* 46 (March 1972): 136.

18. Ibid., p. 137.

19. Joseph M. Powers, *Spirit and Sacrament: The Humanizing Experience* (New York: Seabury Press, 1973), p. 27.

20. Raymond E. Brown, "'Who Do Men Say That I Am?'—Modern Scholarship on Gospel Christology," *Horizons* 1 (Fall 1974): 35-50.

21. Karl Rahner, "Anonymous Christians," *Theological Investigations*, vol. 6, trans. Karl-H. and Boniface Kruger (Baltimore: Helicon Press, 1969), p. 393.

22. Karl Rahner, "Man (Anthropology), III. Theological," *Sacramentum Mundi: An Encyclopedia of Theology*, vol. 3, ed. Karl Rahner et al (New York: Herder and Herder, 1969), p. 370.

23. Gabriel Moran, *The Present Revelation: The Search for Religious Foundations* (New York: Herder and Herder, 1972), p. 273.

24. John Knox, *The Humanity and Divinity of Christ: A Study of Pattern in Christology* (Cambridge University Press, 1967), pp. 73-74.

25. Gustavo Gutierrez, *A Theology of Liberation: History, Politics and Salvation*, trans., ed. Caridad Inda and John Eagleson (Maryknoll: Orbis Books, 1973), p. 226.

26. Aloys Grillmeier, *Christ in Christian Tradition: From the Apostolic Age to Chalcedon (451)*, trans. J.S. Bowden (New York: Sheed and Ward, 1965), p. 493.

27. Sister Mary Finn, letter of March 5, 1976.

5 Christianity and the Human Race

WHAT HAPPENS to the notion of church in contemporary theology? Stated simply, it becomes more expansive and lightsome on the one hand, more profound and religious on the other.

There has been an enormous shift in the theory of church—and following it a shift in official Catholic statements—because there has been an enormous shift in the experience of people. The strongly institutional church shaped in reaction to the Reformation was preserved intact long beyond its time, so that only recently has the facade collapsed. We are living through a wrenching transition period. Baroque Catholicism is behind us, while what is next is not clear.

Actually, there is no eternal essence of church, no blueprint for what church could or must be. In each age, as history shows, the church changes, according to the way most members articulate their religious experience. "It becomes what its leaders and its people choose to make of it."[1]

THE CHURCH YESTERDAY

The church we were brought up in was heavily authoritarian. That it still is that way in our awareness is evident from the frequent use of the traditional phrase, "The Church says . . ."—where *church* obviously means the hierarchy. This is church on the civil or military model: to teach is to decree and to govern is to make laws. To believe is to accept and obey. It is a church where revelation is primarily a deposit of truths confided to an infallible higher power, and where sacraments are channels of grace supervised by the same power. Such a church is the ordinary means of salvation. Those outside have a chance by dint of invincible ignorance and baptism of desire.

This kind of church developed within a particular historical matrix. Four centuries ago an apparently unified Christendom was shattered by the Reformers. A frightened and defensive Rome tightened up doctrine and discipline at Trent. The one true church was a voiceless membership firmly in the grip of an educated elite—because it was a parallel to what was going on in secular society. It was a damaged but triumphalistic fortress, staunchly guarding its truths and sacraments, and demanding full submission from converts. It was a juridical church, preserving law and order by decree and sanction.

From 1550 to 1950, Dulles comments, Roman Catholicism tended toward "*total* institution—one that exists for its own sake and serves others only by aggrandizing itself."[2] Not that structure is bad. Any human assembly has to be organized. But the "institutional elements in the Church must ultimately be justified by their capacity to express or strengthen the Church as a community of life, witness, and service, a community that reconciles and unites men in the grace of Christ."[3]

Many factors contributed to exaggerating the institutional in the Catholic Church. In self-awareness, for instance, it is but a short step from having a divine commission to possessing a divine nature. Thus a metaphor like the Mystical Body of Christ could be taken in some literal way, intensifying the idea that the Church was already a divine body, even with bureaus and committees bearing titles like "Sacred Congregation of Rites." A church working out of a primarily institutional viewpoint "could easily substitute the official Church for God, and this would be a form of idolatry."[4] The pope then becomes one who speaks as if he alone, apart from bishops, experts, and other people, has access to divine information. Church laws tend to supersede persons, and the priorities of a sacred caste tend to precede the needs of the membership.

The institutional developments of the post-Trent church grew out of a self-understanding traditional in the West. As the new chosen people, supplanting the Jews, "the Christian people were situated at the center of world history." To them — and thus to the officials — was entrusted the world's truth and salvation. By an accident of history the church that saw itself as the one and only legitimate religious agency found itself to be European at the time that Europe was discovering and exploring new worlds. Hence the cross was planted on foreign shores along with Christian flags. And traditional church teaching "legitimated the colonial invasion of America, Africa, and Asia . . . The white man's conquest of the continents was regarded as God's providential design to prepare the spread of the Christian Gospel."[5]

Nevertheless, the cold hard center of an institutional model did not prevent the anti-Reformation church from being an alma mater, a warm nursing mother, a Holy Mother Church. Millions lived and died, encouraged by it and strengthened within it and sanctified to the end. Even today this aggressive kind of church provides a zone of stability in a swiftly changing world and it can engender a comforting sense of corporate identity, along with a high visibility and lifelong loyalty. Its style of teaching, governing, and ministering, however, belongs to a particular age of history.

THE CHURCH TODAY

The military and regal style becomes oppressive today; it alienates. Ours is an age of universal schooling and TV. Our contemporary awareness demands an open, humane assembly where each has some voice, where presumed absolutes will not break someone's back, where accountability and honesty are elementary expectations. Evidently some changes are going on, from local parish to Rome, that correspond to today's experience.

Contemporary theology, working out the implications of Mystery Present, sets Church in perspective. Since God is present to each person and since one's Yes is the acceptance of salvation, the real issue of Church is no longer whether salvation is possible in or out of it.

Instead, if *church* in a general way can refer to the human association or agency through which salvation comes and is articulated, then we could say that the human race itself is the primary church and that human life is the primary sacrament. Any other churches and any other sacraments will be particularizations of these. Neither Rome nor Geneva nor Salt Lake City will be the unit of measure for religion. Nothing less than the human race will suffice. Thus the norm of salvation will be the Human Race Church. For not all men, presumably, are called to be Christians or Buddhists, but all men are called to be Godians or Mysterians.

To talk about the Human Race Church, of course, is a non-technical way to indicate "universal salvation." Theologians today have no difficulty assuming salvation available to each person, apart from church affiliation. This stand seems well supported in the biblical experience and surely in modern experience.

In the New Testament, for example, there is the much-quoted 1 Timothy 2:1-6, where Paul refers to "God our Savior, who desires all men to be saved." Whether we come to Him through Hinduism or through Judaism, in fact "there is one God" of all. This largeness of view comes out again in Acts 10: 34-35, when Peter encounters the pagan Cornelius: "Truly I perceive that God shows no partiality, but in every nation any one who fears him and does what is right is acceptable to him." Then in the Gospels Jesus is remembered as having crossed sectarian boundaries easily. For instance, he flouted convention when he sat alone at the well with a woman, and a non-Jewish one at that. Despite her five marriages, he took her most seriously.

The New Testament Jesus drinking as heartily with sinners as with nice people would fit into modern pluralistic society, where we are not surprised to find honesty, compassion, or responsibility everywhere, apart from church allegiance. In fact, some of the great movements in moral awareness have emerged not from churches but from "secular" society. Religion had to learn its lesson from outsiders, for instance, in the area of modern systematic self-criticism, in freedom of research, in honesty in scholarship, in respect for people with whom one disagrees, in equality of all before the law, and so on. "Catholics had to struggle before these ideals were acknowledged in the Church."[6]

The civil rights movement in our country is a massive example of moral progress which got going without the Catholic Church. It confronts head-on the same basic social issue that is the underlying thrust of moral movements such as anti-war and women's liberation: can I really accept people as persons? Historians a thousand years from now may well point back to our age as the time of a quantum leap in moral consciousness. No matter how unfulfilled these movements are now or may be, results already achieved, like our civil rights legislation, are absolutely new in the history of mankind.

Today, then, no matter how much we may aspire to a new Christendom, we can only presume that pluralism and secularity are here to stay. The truth is that after two thousand years of Christianity, only twenty percent of the planet's population seems to be inscribed as explicitly Christian. Being Christian therefore can scarcely be the norm of salvation; otherwise, most people would be lost. Today it is with silent horror that we read Augustine to see how ready he was to consign the non-baptized to perdition.

Contemporary theology, therefore, is convinced that Mystery is present to each man, available for his Yes. Whatever religions can mean, they cannot go against our fundamental, life-tested feeling that each person counts. In the biblical experience this was picturesquely phrased: "Are not two sparrows sold for a penny? And not one of them will fall to the ground without your Father's will" (Matthew 10:29).

In our time the Catholic Church has officially taken a step toward declaring itself a friend of all religious people. It has thus abandoned its aim of the last four centuries, to be a fortress of chosen ones to which earnest searchers outside finally come. In documents of Vatican II we find, intermingled, strands of both "new" and "old" theologies (after all, these are compromise documents, voted on by a convention of three thousand). But one significant passage signalizes an altered self-awareness among the bishops. In the *Dogmatic Constitution on the Church*, where they easily could have declared that the "Church of Christ" is solely the Roman Catholic Church—as has been traditional—they instead go on record thus: "This Church, constituted and organized in the world as a society, subsists in the Catholic Church."[7] To leave it ambiguous this way is an "epochal decision."[8] It recognizes how the Church can be present beyond Roman boundaries.

The distinction here is important. No longer must other Christian groups be considered necessarily as dying branches broken off the one true tree. Accepting the convictions of modern man, Vatican II seems to admit that Christ's true church could have diverse concrete realizations.

Not only did Vatican II accept the fact of other Christian churches, but it also affirmed universal salvation, using especially the biblical image "kingdom of God." For example: "On this earth that kingdom is already present in mystery. When the Lord returns, it will be brought into full flower."[9] All men are eligible for this kingdom, by the very fact that they were born, for it is the Human Race Church.

Exploiting the distinction between kingdom and (Christian) Church, McBrien comes to conclusions like this: "membership in the Church does not guarantee affiliation with either the present or the future Kingdom, nor does life apart from the Church indicate exclusion from the Kingdom."[10] This would let us say, for instance, that the Church of Christ is a smaller circle within the huge circle, the Human Race Church.

> The Church is no longer to be conceived as the center of God's plan of salvation. Not all men are called to membership in the Church, nor is such membership a sign of present salvation or a guarantee of future salvation. The central reality is not the Church but the Kingdom of God. . . . The

> Kingdom of God is the reign and rule of God in
> Christ, and it comes into being wherever and
> whenever men love one another and accept one
> another's burdens with a spirit of compassion,
> concern, generosity, and sensitivity. All men are
> called to the Kingdom; not all men are called to
> the Church.[11]

The Christian Church is "sign and instrument of the Kingdom
of God." Christians give explicit witness to what happens to
all men everywhere. "It is the Kingdom and not the Church
which is the only theological absolute."[12]

"The real distinction between election to the Church
and election to God's Kingdom," notes Carl Peter, "can
hardly be repeated too often." There is "in fact a real danger
of idolatry in accepting as divine what is in fact not merely
human but sinfully so."[13]

But if authentic salvation is universal, then why bother
to be Christian? People are drawn to the Christian churches
"because they are haunted by the figure of Jesus of Nazareth."
Fiery St. Paul, originally a persecutor of Christians and then
suddenly an enthusiastic apostle, is an example of adult
election or vocation. "The mystery of election is at the heart
of the Christian understanding of life and history."[14]

But why then be a Catholic Christian? To be a Christian
is to join a small circle within the Human Race Church,
and to be a Catholic is to join a still smaller circle within
the Christian circle.

On the concrete personal level, nearly all the Catholics
we know have not consciously chosen to be baptized Catholics.
Our experience is like Rahner's:

> I was born a Catholic because I was born and bap-

tized in a believing environment. I trust in God that this faith passed on by tradition has turned into my own decision — into a real belief — and that I am a Catholic Christian even in my innermost being. This, in the last analysis, remains God's secret.[15]

All this, one might object, is a long way from what we were told in school, about how we were the salt of the earth and the city on the mountain top. Catholics are now the same as Protestants, and Christians are only humanists. What's happened to our identity? "Identity," replies Gray, "has not in fact been lost, but its meaning has been decisively re-interpreted." It is one thing to understand yourself "over-against other people in terms of your differences from them and quite another to understand yourself together with them in terms of what is shared in common." It's one thing to see yourself "as being at the center of all things" but entirely "another to understand yourself as being at the service of all."[16]

Belief versus unbelief, then, is not the ready distinction between Christian Church and the rest of mankind. Rather, it is a difference of explicitness in articulating religious experience. "What the Christian community has to offer by way of distinctiveness is . . . a peculiar kind of conscious-ness."[17] It is a matter of a new awareness, thanks to the Good News. "The Church alone is conscious of the redemptive mystery that goes on everywhere." It is the Christian who is "aware of what goes on in him and in others: he believes that in Christ the universal mystery of redemption has been made known to him." It is "the Christian alone" who "explicitly acknowledges this mystery which is omnipresent in the lives of men." It is the Christian "who has become totally conscious of who he is."[18]

Within the perspective of universal salvation through a Human Race Church, therefore, the Christian Church stands as a reminder or witness. It should radiate (even if in fact it sometimes obscures) the experience that life is worthwhile, that our living together is divinely significant, that the pain of growth and death can be healing and liberating—as the process proves in Mystery's work in Jesus.

This work of radiating is concentrated in the sacraments. Liturgy is the event where any church is most itself, most visible, most explicit. It is the common public prayer of people who already have had religious experience, who assemble with their spokesmen to renew their awareness of Mystery Present, to re-evoke and express it, and to react within it. Liturgy is a celebration of Mystery, as present now as in the transformation of Jesus. Liturgy is basically the prayer of praise and thanksgiving, with the eucharistic service as its most characteristic form.

But even at its most actualized in the memorial meal of the Mass, the Christian assembly is not preoccupied with itself. "It should celebrate not only the wonderful things which have happened and are happening to Christians, but also the wonderful things which have happened and continue to happen in the lives of all men." For "All of life and the lives of all are included in the eucharistic activity of God."[19]

The church, however, is not a community left to huddle happily behind protective walls. It is also a community sharing the world as it stands, a checkerboard of good alongside evil. Today there is the growing conviction that even when pointing back to the Jesus past and pointing forward to the Second Coming, the church is surely not outside the nitty-gritty world. Rather, it is definitely "an institution *within* it, criticizing it, having a critical liberating task in regard to it."[20] As a body the believing community in America, for example, must share the hard questions asked by other national critics: When does the American dream turn into a nightmare? What is consumerism doing to our lives? If we are going to give our children and our leisure over to television, what will we do about the quality and level of what we see for hours on end?

Being a cultural, social, economic, and political critic may seem something new for Christianity, which has long thought of itself as part of the establishment in any society. Even today in the United States, despite separation of church and state, religion is expected to be seen but not heard from—perhaps in exchange for perquisites like tax-exemption, military chaplaincies, clergy discounts. Some people still wonder why so little was said by the churches, collectively, against the loss of lives in the undeclared Vietnam War—when it seems easy today to take a public stand against abortion. Only slowly is the Christian community finding its eyes to perceive oppressive political and economic structures, and its voice to call for radical change.

Finally there is the missionary role of the Christian assembly, whereby it invites outsiders explicitly to share its vision and experience. Of course a missionary program will depend on the assembly's view of church. Since all men have access to Mystery before the missionary arrives, his concern for conversion has to be larger than inscribing names in a register. "Conversion in the biblical and theological sense means first of all a turning to God, rather than to any particular community of men." A missioner's preoccupation should be the relation of each person with Mystery and with each other. "As regards men of other faiths, the Christian can assist them to become converted to God within the framework of the religion they already profess."[21] This would indeed be the mystagogical approach, making most of each person's direct relation to Mystery.

A missionary is the mystagogue who sets out to share with people his religious experience. He hopes that the Easter message speaks to them. He respects what he finds and brings no pre-determined idea of the form their Christianity will assume. "He must allow himself to be told by his hearers, since they, not he, are the new Church that is taking root."[22] In this connection, note Bishop Maanicus's statement at a recent Roman Synod concerning evangelization in Africa: "We wish to reclaim our cultural rituals, predating colonialism, as a way that allows us to find God again with the mediation of our ancestors."[23]

THE CHURCH TOMORROW

Meanwhile what is going on back home? Church there too is human interchange. We live out and reflect upon and celebrate what is of ultimate concern, finding our strongest hope in what Mystery did in Jesus. Structurally church is basically persons-in-relation. To achieve such a model, Moran urges, we need "some alternative to the bureaucratic model" that we are working with. "The basic communal unit of church would ideally be larger than two but probably not larger than twelve or fifteen." In such a "personalizing unit" each individual can receive the "affection, support, and solace" he needs, while the size limitation permits "direct participation by every member in the life of the group."[24]

Yet an intimate group left to itself loses its identity and energy, and obviously cannot organize to deal with political and social issues. But the small primary group can be the living cell in some larger body. "The need is not only for small groups but a connection between small groups." A network is formed when the cells locate "decision-making power in a central (not higher) body."[25] Even though there are various roles and ministries, all are members and all share in the dialogue.

This cell model may seem utopian and inefficient. But it may turn out to be a common realistic solution for those who want religion but who do not want to be anonymous parishioners ushered into benches from which they watch the backs of peoples' heads. Now that Catholics have been aroused from their dogmatic slumber (rudely awakened to learn, for instance, that Catholics don't have to eat fish on Friday, and that maybe it never was a mortal sin to miss Mass on Sunday), and now that young people especially are wondering whether they want to ally themselves with a parish, we should not discard the cell model as being unworkable. Living-room religion apparently does work. It goes on today but on no official basis. It seems to have been the structure Jesus worked within, as at the Last Supper.

It is also true that the New Testament represents Jesus presiding at a religious event where five thousand people were assembled. That is comparable to the situation when the pope conducts a ceremony in St. Peter's Square or when he goes to a foreign land and leads a liturgy in a ball park or stadium. But the ordinary religious life of Christians would seem best nourished in small, interpersonal groupings. Church should be the cordial place where the butcher, the baker, and the garbage man all feel free to testify. In a mystagogical church all share priestly and prophetic roles by their very orientation to Mystery. What people need is "a realization that they are all prophets who must speak their convictions with passion and must test their wisdom in the community."[26]

There is the danger of disillusionment, of course, when we attempt to make church a fellowship in fact. We can expect too much from ourselves and from each other. Dulles cautions that "Christians commonly experience the Church more as a companionship of fellow travelers on the same journey than as a union of lovers dwelling in the same home."[27]

Despite this and many other risks, we cannot give up searching for alternative structures that free people to be their religious selves together. We may have no choice in the matter, whether to search further or not. For it seems that we have not seen the worst yet, so that some day we may be driven to get at the gut issues. For the present we will likely continue to feel daring because we have moved surface components around.

In theory, anyhow, no matter what the level of practice, church is organized concern for others and search for God. Far from intruding upon each individual's awareness of Mystery in contemplation, it frees and develops such awareness. We are irrevocably social and want to share our depth experiences. But thus far, nowadays, to talk seriously about ultimate issues, you have to join a discussion group or to be a Pentecostal. Maybe (as in Moran's church of cells), some way will be found for serious people to regularize their sharing, which they conclude with a eucharistic meal.

The church of Mystery Present was not destined to remain (as it pretty much now is in fact) an aggregate of isolated families and scattered individuals. Christians are devotees of Mystery but are not separate devotees. "Christianity is essentially both God and people, community, and it is no more conceivable without people than it is without

God."[28] There may be Christian hermits but not separated individual Christians. Union is a mark of Christian groups, where, if anywhere on earth, people are aware that they are thereby also in touch with Mystery. Christianity is "a religion which teaches that he who tries to receive God's self-offer without offering himself to his neighbor, who tries to love God without loving his neighbor, is attempting the impossible."[29]

Christianity, then, embraces the tension between the vertical and the horizontal, between the individual and the believing community, between the community and the world. No one can give up hoping and working for the day when all people can sit down to the heavenly banquet. Until then, we have to push for just social and economic structures that promote brotherhood. And we have to push for the church that affords an experience similar to that reported about the two disciples on the way to Emmaus. They enjoyed table fellowship with a stranger, and it was only after the warmth of the encounter that they realized that Jesus had been present to them. "Were not our hearts burning within us?"

Whatever guidelines and injunctions and functions and edifices are helpful for church, the final test would be the exclamation of the apostles at the transfiguration: "Lord, it is good for us to be here!"

NOTES

1. Avery Dulles, *Models of the Church* (Garden City: Doubleday, 1974), p. 188.

2. Ibid., p. 39.

3. Ibid., p. 42.

4. Ibid., pp. 183-184.

5. Gregory Baum, "Theology After Auschwitz: A Conference Report," *The Ecumenist* 12 (July-August 1974): 73.

6. Gregory Baum, *Man Becoming: God in Secular Language* (New York: Herder and Herder, 1970), p. x.

7. *Dogmatic Constitution on the Church*, no. 8, in *The Documents of Vatican II*, ed. Walter M. Abbott (New York: Guild Press, 1966), p. 23.

8. Dulles, *Models of the Church*, p. 130.

9. *Pastoral Constitution on the Church in the Modern World*, no. 39, in *The Documents of Vatican II*, ed. Walter M. Abbott (New York: Guild Press, 1966), pp. 237-238.

10. Richard P. McBrien, *Do We Need the Church?* (New York: Harper and Row, 1969), p. 94.

11. Ibid., p. 14-15.

12. Ibid., p. 15.

13. Carl J. Peter, "Why Catholic Theology Needs Future Talk Today," Proceedings of the Catholic Theological Society of America 27 (1972): 158.

14. McBrien, *Do We Need the Church?*, p. 171.

15. Karl Rahner, "Thoughts on the Possibility of Belief Today," *Theological Investigations*, vol. 5, trans. Karl-H. Kruger (Baltimore: Helicon Press, 1966), p. 4.

16. Donald P. Gray, "Sacramental Consciousness-Raising," *Worship* 46 (March 1972): 133.

17. Ibid., p. 135.

18. Baum, *Man Becoming*, p. 64.

19. Gray, "Sacramental Consciousness-Raising," p. 139.

20. Johannes B. Metz, *Theology of the World*, trans. William Glen-Doepel (New York: Herder and Herder, 1969), p. 115.

21. Avery Dulles, "Current Trends in Mission Theology," *Theology Digest* 20 (Spring 1972): 33.

22. Ibid., p. 34.

23. Donald R. Campion, "Synod Jottings II," *America* 131 (19 October 1974): 206.

24. Gabriel Moran, *The Present Revelation: The Search for Religious Foundations* (New York: Herder and Herder, 1972), p. 300.

25. Ibid., p. 301.

26. Ibid., p. 228.

27. Dulles, *Models of the Church*, p. 57.

28. Norbert J. Rigali, "On Christian Ethics," *Chicago Studies* 10 (Fall 1971): 230.

29. Ibid., p. 232.

6 Mystery in Living and Liturgy

W E HAVE STATED that contemporary theology can be both liberating and challenging. It expects us to trust in and work with our own experience. It points to a renewal and restoration based on each individual person's vocation: to be attentive to the intimations in his depths. The institutions of all religions must assume this experience, celebrate it, and foster it. What is involved here, then, is a program of mysticism, a mystagogy. But it is an everyman's "mysticism that leads to a religious experience which indeed many suppose that they never could discover in themselves." Directions or prescriptions are useful in this program only so far as they help each one to "become his own teacher of mysticism."[1]

INTERIOR EXPERIENCE

Mystagogy returns today as something new in the Catholic Church, which during the past four centuries has suspected the charismatic element and kept it under tight control. With the rite of sacramental penance common up to recently, for example, people going into the confessional box seemed generally convinced that they were reconciled to God if they received absolution from the confessor, and that they were not forgiven by God if the confessor refused to say the absolution formula. Penitents would take as settled, also, the confessor's decision on conscience problems.

One consequence is that we grew up in a church where "experience" was mainly something that went on in our heads. The fundamental factors of religion were strongly intellectualized. Thus revelation was the book of divine words, and tradition was their accurate transmission and correct interpretation. Belief was assent to propositions. The premium was on words. Even today some, if not many, wish that Catholic schools would still require students to memorize approved formulas. We are still printing catechisms old and new, and we are putting a lot of hope in a National Catechetical Directory.

But to stress the rationalist — and therefore controllable — side of experience is not merely a Catholic phenemenon. All churches concerned with orthodoxy have been defensive and even repressive about texts and formulations. Over the centuries for both Catholics and Protestants, for instance, Christian revelation has been something fragile, guarded jealously and transmitted gingerly. The faithful were to accept the Tradition (or the Book) as it came, without alteration. Then, too, there is the inhibiting factor of competitive, technological Western culture, especially in the Anglo tradition. So that today in North America, getting people back in touch with themselves is in fact a new industry: counselling, encounter groups, psychotherapy.

Despite the fact that mystagogy looks new to us, to expect people to have confidence in their religious experience seems justified by early Christian tradition. To take a striking example: St. Paul, as one who had never met the man Jesus, seemed hugely confident about his personal experiences, not all of which seem to have been backed up by community memories.

Actually, the focus on one's interior experience as a valid foundation for religion has been a trend among professional theologians for more than a century, since Schleiermacher in particular. But until recently the trend remained largely Protestant. Today, though, we are not surprised to read Tracy's statement: "I believe that a contemporary Christian theology can best be described as philosophical reflection upon common human experience and upon the Christian fact."[2] The Christian fact, of course, is especially what is recorded in the New Testament. By common human experience he means "the religious dimension present in everyday and scientific experience," which he would investigate by phenomenological reflection.[3] Such an approach seems to signalize the fact that it is now respectable in Catholic professional circles to take our experiences most seriously.

What we have been at in these discussions on Mystery Present is a survey limited to some recent Catholic writers. The story could be told as effectively from a study of Protestant theologians, and in some ways even more interestingly told from a study of humanistic psychologists. The point we have been making is that some prominent contemporary theologians proceed on the fundamental conviction that Mystery is present, available for each man's Yes. If the ancient formulations and presumed eternal truths do not correspond to our religious awareness, then they will have to be re-interpreted. For "we must look to human experience for whatever is to be found."[4]

But of course contemporary discernment of Mystery has not flouted the past. The recent four centuries of a defensive theology and discipline were not characteristic of other eras of the Catholic Church. Thus mystagogy is a rediscovery through the contemporary method of phenomenological analysis, of dwelling on the contents of our experience.

Experience, as it is discussed here refers to a whole-person awareness. It includes not only the clear-edged part of ourselves that we have words for, but also the vast area of feeling that itself seems to be the surface for elusive depths we can only guess at dumbly. Human awareness is many-leveled and seemingly unlimited.

For most of us, perhaps, to be fully aware may come only after much purification. We may be so conditioned by our past, we may perceive through so many filters, that we may scarcely know what actually we ourselves really think and feel. So that when contemporary writers urge us to explore the religious side of our experience, we may not be reading our depths but mainly remembering words we were told and which we only take as ours. However, to be sensitive to this problem is already to be solving it.

If we are attentive, we discover our graced moments. We say good-bye to grandmother—and suddenly we are somehow overwhelmed by the goodness of the universe. We sit on a rock watching the waves, impressed by something unending. We hurry away from a visit to the hospital, fearing our own vulnerability and transience. Whatever route opens up to us, we are led to affirm an unlimit and beyondness ever out of reach.

In our depths, then, we have hints of some ultimate, ungraspable and unnamed. Such experience leads us to faith but does not coerce us to say Yes. From the community's store of symbols we get the name "God" to indicate the experience. Christians maintain that history (read of course in faith) provides the most real interpretation of all.

The danger of delusion in community tradition is that the exterior articulations of the religious impulse can remain behind on their own, as lovely shells, while the life within has left. Religion can become family tradition and social convention, or a profession and mere job. Contemporary theology reminds us that through traditional formulations we have dimmed if not lost our sense of wonder. It insists that the very purpose of Christian community is to foster and celebrate our religious intimations. The "experience of God," says Rahner, "really constitutes the very heart and centre of Christianity itself." This experience of God, "in its most radical form," is in our depths.[5] The emphasis here, clearly, is not on creeds, biblical texts, programs, or buildings—but on our mystical experience. For genuine religious life we start with our religious experience and remain in touch with it.

To show further how the business of Christianity is this primal experience in which we affirm God, we can look at how this works out in two major areas, theology and liturgy.

THEOLOGY

Personalist theologies assume that all Christian dogmas and doctrine reduce to the notion—and the experience—of Mystery Present. This emphasis may contradict our stereotype of theology as learned labor conducted in libraries in order to produce intricate and logical discussions of abstruse topics. Whereas the truth of the matter is that Christian theology should be the easiest knowledge of all. The community of course cherishes its experts and specialists as critics and guides, but theology has to be community dialogue that respects the testimony of everyone, including the unschooled. "Christianity, among all religions, says the least in detail since it always says the one thing."[6] Rahner further states that, "in spite of the complicated appearance of its dogmatic and moral theology," Christianity really says "something simple which all particular dogmas of Christianity articulate in some way." And what is this which Christianity really proclaims?

> Nothing else, after all, than that the great Mystery remains eternally a mystery, but that this mystery wishes to communicate Himself in absolute self-communication—as the infinite, incomprehensible and inexpressible Being whose name is God, as self-giving nearness—to the human soul in the midst of its experience of its own finite emptiness.[7]

The one fundamental message of Christianity, then, is that God lovingly is here and now present. Contemporary theology is at pains to show that this is what all the great symbols of tradition point to: grace, creation, Incarnation, redemption, salvation, revelation.

Grace, in the preaching tradition we grew up on, came off graphically as something Christ merited and stored up, and which flowed to us through the sacraments especially. But today we realize that this mechanized picture is the final stage of a process that began as a reflection on the relationship between God and man. Today's stress on Mystery Present makes it less necessary to visualize a third something between us and God. Rather, we are immersed in presence and have only to say Yes. This truth is effectively expressed by the indwelling images from the New Testament. Contemporary theology has "returned to the biblical vision that grace is primarily God's mercy and love for us, his living and loving presence reaching out to the very core of our existence."[8] The term *grace* then points to our experience of transcendent benevolence in life, of forgiveness, of meaning in a sometimes absurd world.

God's presence as loving gift, of course, can be understood as personal to each of us. However, as the biblical experience of both Old and New Testaments indicates, Mystery is vividly present also to the community. For the very dynamism of divine presence is unifying—Mystery to man, man to Mystery, man to man. Thus in our era of heightened awareness, people who find their economic and social structures oppressive can experience Mystery as a liberating force in their lives, in their struggle to achieve dignity and brotherhood.

Creation points to Mystery's ongoing self-communication, as a here-and-now presence in time and space. Birds and bees happen when God expresses Himself on our level. Creation is the productive way Mystery can be present. Theology today is not concerned about locating the first blackbird or the first dawn, nor does it find particularly helpful the classical statement that creation is "from nothing" (though the formula does remind us creatures that we are not God). But for our time the emphasis should be that God is all that we are. We cannot escape His love; we are in and of Him.

Creation is especially our self-creation, the process whereby we grow toward a Yes to ourselves, to others, to Mystery. This means we struggle to remove the obstacles blocking the flow of universal love energy. In our individual life and in social and public life we reform and build structures that clear away the fear and agression that block union. To create actually is to bring about the justice and the community of all men—thus to advance God's rule and reign.

To talk of self-creation is in no way to suggest that of

ourselves we can achieve anything. On the contrary, we can understand the universe only as God's ongoing initiative and luring. So that when we are most forceful in our purpose and effort, we are only accepting gifts, including the gift of being enabled to accept.

Incarnation originally refers to man's creation, though the term has become a technical word about Jesus. Man, all people, are what happen when Mystery, so to speak, extrudes Itself. "If God wills to become non-God," Rahner suggests, "man comes to be."[9] All people are divine, with the man Jesus truly representing His own kind. Some theologians today would make Jesus unique among us through the totality of His openness and surrender to the Father. While Christians see Jesus as the climax of God's self-giving, creation and Incarnation are actually not separate acts but are "two moments" of that one "process of God's self-renunciation and self-expression into what is other than himself."[10]

Redemption verbalizes our experience of return and reconciliation in Mystery's presence. This experience can remain within or can be ritualized in community. Taken in the original New Testament meaning, redemption does not need the original sin mythology that classical theology of the West made so much of. Some theologians return to the tradition that "the first and most basic motive for the Incarnation was not the blotting-out of sin" committed by Adam or by anyone else, but that Jesus's coming was "already the goal of the divine freedom even apart from any divine foreknowledge of freely incurred guilt."[11] Redemption is a symbol to emphasize God's presence to His own, even when we turn away to sin.

Salvation also tells about Mystery Present now. It is true that we speak of heaven as coming after death, and of a second coming. But those are mythological elements indicating some final form of salvation. The truth is that God is alive now and that salvation goes on already. Personalist theology insists that salvation is Mystery's self-offer to us in experience, which offer we accept with our Yes. Heaven, then, is already begun. For salvation is "in the deepest sense, God himself."[12]

We may call Jesus our savior in so far as Mystery's action was most visible in him, in his being raised from the dead and being transformed. Thus we would be saved (helped in saying our Yes) by Jesus to the extent that we are illumined and encouraged by him. But, strictly speaking, the primary savior is Mystery Present, the Father Unoriginate.

> God himself *is* the salvation and at the same time the power to receive the salvation in such a way that this salvation really is God himself, and God remains not only the ultimate Cause but the real content as well of this salvation.[13]

To say, of course, that salvation is already begun, that somehow heaven is here on earth, is in no way to close our eyes to the private and public evil we are immersed in. The Bible seems to affirm the orientation suggested by science: that salvation is also to evolve. Although God's kingdom is already started, it must go through a long process to arrive at some completed form that is symbolized by the Second Coming, when the lion will lie down with the lamb. Human structures that unerringly promote universal brotherhood have to be developed. Nothing we yet know or even can imagine will deliver the justice and peace that have to be the basis for full human community. All, and Christians surely, have to labor toward's God's future, to reflect and devise, to work and maybe even to bring about revolution, as part of the process of advancing the kingdom.

Revelation, more than any other symbol, registers sensitively the orientation of a theology and the world vision it elaborates. Up to Vatican II, classical revelation was a body of sacred propositions, the Bible, guarded and interpreted by church authorities for the assent of the faithful. The Bible was literally the word of the Lord, directly infused in the minds of prophets and heard by the apostles from Jesus. Today, however, Scripture experts and theologians reject such a simplistic view. It makes God's work seem inert and outside of us, and something finished two thousand years ago. It allows talk about how God is dead. Furthermore, it would make being a loyal Christian a matter of living in the past.

Contemporary theology has no unanimous theory of revelation,[14] but many understand it as Mystery's presence to us now, on the model of inter-personal relationship. Characteristic could be this description: "Revelation occurs wherever and whenever man has an experience of the presence of God."[15] Revelation is "not information about God," nor is it "information about the past." It simply isn't information. Rather, it is God's own "self-revelation and hence the initiation of man into a new self-consciousness."[16] To be aware of revelation is like falling in love; there is no new content or data, but there is an enlargement of horizon. We find ourselves reaching out to a wholeness and a totality; we find life has meaning; we feel that there must be a forever where our search for unity has a term.

The ongoing intimate contact between God and each person is primary revelation. The exterior expression of that experience is secondary revelation. This includes every kind of behavior and verbalization, and constitutes history. According to this view, for example, the Bible is not primary revelation but the early Church's articulation of its primary experience.

Now whatever point personalist reflection starts from it ends up with Mystery Present. In this way theology is the "'science' of Mystery as such" It is not a science in that it develops more and more details and distinctions, but because it is a "human activity in which man, even at the level of conscious thought, relates the multiplicity of the realities, experiences, and ideas in his life to that mystery, ineffable and obscure, which we call God."[17] Thus, no matter how many mysteries or truths or dogmas Christianity can discern,

> there is, and there can be, only one single absolute mystery in the strictest sense of the term, namely God himself and in relation to him all those aspects under which man with his finite knowledge has to conceive of God to himself are specified in the same manner by this character of the *mysterium*.[18]

Theology, doctrine and dogma — any form of reflection — directs us to our experience of Mystery Present.

LITURGY

"How can we get people to church?" seems a preoccupation of parish workers. Now that hellfire is no longer a sanction to back up the old Sunday obligation, and people have seen changes made in an unchanging tradition, we are embarked on an apparently endless search for rites that satisfy. Re-

forms attempted so far seem restricted to matters like new
Mass texts and revised readings. We seem still to operate on
the classical assumption about the great importance of words,
and of right words, in a church where experience was mainly
in the head. Our parish idioms are revealing: the celebrant
"reads" or "says" Mass, while the lay people "hear" it.

Reform is in danger of being superficial, however, on a
far more fundamental level. It can be "a superficiality that
can arise most particularly from not dealing with the radical
situation of man's religious experience." To Gallen, "Liturgy
is a moment of religious experience as well as a gathering
together and sacramentalizing of one's life of religious faith
experience . . . and so it is always plunged in the mystery of
God."[19]

Parish workers may labor hard at merchandising and
salesmanship, perhaps even as if that is the missing ingre-
dient. Public relations, however, could prove to be merely
a bandage on a compound fracture—if the major issue is not
also attended to. "The problem of liturgy," says Gallen, "is
quite literally the problem of God."[20] Liturgists simply cannot assume that everyone in a parish, even when he recites
the creed, is really committed to God. Hence Carl Peter
warns that regarding "an ever-increasing number of educated men and women," liturgists have not faced "the central
issue . . . the God-question."[21]

People who seem in early life to have said Yes to a childhood God may later on change their option to Maybe. Some
go to church for the sake of the children, or for the sake of
business and respectability. All these people have depth experiences which a liturgy should address. A group to be
especially aware of are young couples who seem serious,
reflective, and genuinely religious, but who are unhappy
with church services. Regularly they are Catholic school

graduates. Some cease to claim membership in any parish, perhaps dropping in at a Newman center. Others tell how they gave up on the "institutional Church."

Our churches may never fill up again, no matter what changes are made. We might as well make honesty the best policy, leaving the gimmicks and tinsel aside. In shaping a contemporary liturgy for those interested — and for serious people we could hope to interest — the question to keep asking is: How will a service express and interpret, evoke and intensify the depth experience of the assembly members?

To say that experience of God is at the core of liturgy is only part of the story. Liturgy is the prayer of the community, its most explicit awareness of God. To put liturgy in context is to tell the rest of the story. Otherwise, there is the danger of sacramentalism, exaggerating the place of sacraments.

Since each person has direct access to Mystery Present, every moment and every occasion can lead to God. Our relation to Mystery does not start with liturgy; liturgy, in fact, celebrates what goes on the rest of the time. The presence of God to everyone is also the basis for ecumenism; no religion has a monopoly on God. Actually "the first and foremost means of grace is life itself," with the consequence that "the sacramental Church which is meant to serve and intensify this mystery becomes of secondary importance."[22]

> For what God is doing through the sacraments in an explicit fashion, he is doing in a more implicit manner through the words and gestures that are part of life itself. There is a good dogmatic basis for the shocking statement that there may be more communion taking place in the tavern on Saturday night than in the church on Sunday morning.[23]

Grace—Mystery's presence as gift—is rampant in the universe, not captured by nor confined to one religion, nor to seven sacraments. "God is *everywhere* as the world's grace."[24] Mystery is for everyone, so that "as long as we don't say 'No' to him, then our whole life . . . is sacred liturgy."[25]

Thus contemporary reflection reverses the tendency of classical theology to consider Christians as leaving church services as "loaded with God's grace," going "back into a godless world." Instead, we come to liturgy "from a world filled with God" already (yet where His presence may be heavily veiled) to a community celebration where grace reaches "complete self-awareness."[26] A renewed sacramental theology stresses that liturgy is continuous with daily living and church is continuous with the secular world. "The sacraments appointed by Christ reveal to us how God offers transformation to men through the ordinary events of their lives."[27]

CONCLUSION

The worldview of theology today is indeed different from the classical worldview, where man was a natural being cut off by a chasm from the super-natural. Christ earned graces that could be brought over the chasm by sacraments. The faithful arrived at the house of the Lord from a God-less environment. God up there was brought down on the altar by the priest's words of consecration.

By contrast, a contemporary theologian like Powers insists that "our sacramental religion does not 'deliver God,'" since to begin with He is already here, waiting for us to be aware of Him. There is no God apart that we can get outside of in order to inspect or to pray to. There is nothing separated that needs connecting by sacraments or graces. "There is no object-God in the possession of the ritual or minister of the sacraments."[28] Aware of our depth experience, we assemble in order to give Mystery Present a name in worship.

Doctrine and dogma are significant in so far as they may help us to live our lives and conduct our liturgy with greater understanding. We appreciate better that it is Mystery which we experience, and which we reflect on and pray to. We will know better how "we are speaking of an unfathomable depth revealed to us through a depth in our own lives which transcends any of our own action and achievement."[29]

Theology today, then, urges us to value and trust our depth experiences. We sense intimations of a presence that invites us to union and to community. Just as Yahweh was understood as present among the Hebrews like a cloud by day and a fireball by night, so Mystery Present can be felt as drawing us forward from the realm of sin, fear, and greed — into the Promised Land of peace and fellowship.

NOTES

1. Karl Rahner, "Christian Living Formerly and Today," *Theological Investigations*, vol. 7, trans. David Bourke (London: Darton, Longman and Todd, 1971), p. 14.

2. David Tracy, "The Task of Fundamental Theology," *Journal of Religion* 54 (January 1974): 13.

3. Ibid., p. 19.

4. Gabriel Moran, *The Present Revelation: The Search for Religious Foundations* (New York: Herder and Herder, 1972), p. 82.

5. Karl Rahner, "The Experience of God Today," *Theological Investigations*, vol. 11, trans. David Bourke (London: Darton, Longman and Todd, 1974), p. 164.

6. Karl Rahner, "Thoughts on the Possibility of Belief Today,"

Theological Investigations, vol. 5, trans. Karl-H. Kruger (Baltimore: Helicon Press, 1966), p. 10.

7. Ibid., p. 6.

8. Piet Fransen, "Grace, Theologizing and the Humanizing of Man," Proceedings of the Catholic Theological Society of America 27 (1972): 76.

9. Karl Rahner, "On the Theology of the Incarnation," *Theological Investigations*, vol. 4, trans. Kevin Smyth (Baltimore: Helicon Press, 1966), p. 116.

10. Karl Rahner, "Christology within an Evolutionary View of the World," *Theological Investigations*, vol. 5, trans. Karl-H. Kruger (Baltimore: Helicon Press, 1966), pp. 177-178.

11. Ibid., p. 184. Rahner here summarizes the scotist position.

12. Karl Rahner, "Church, Churches and Religions," *Theological Investigations*, vol. 10, trans. David Bourke (New York: Herder and Herder, 1973), p. 34.

13. Ibid.

14. Avery Dulles, "The Problem of Revelation," Proceedings of the Catholic Theological Society of America 29 (1974): 77-106.

15. Richard P. McBrien, *Do We Need the Church?* (New York: Harper and Row, 1969), p. 193.

16. Gregory Baum, *Man Becoming: God in Secular Language* (New York: Herder and Herder, 1970), p. 218.

17. Karl Rahner, "Reflections on Methodology in Theology," *Theological Investigations*, vol. 11, trans. David Bourke (London: Darton, Longman and Todd, 1974), p. 102.

18. Ibid., pp. 105-106.

19. John Gallen, "A Pastoral-Liturgical View of Penance Today," *Worship* 45 (March 1971): 140.

20. Ibid.

21. Carl Peter, "Renewal of Penance and the Problem of God," *Theological Studies* 30 (September 1969), p. 493.

22. Baum, *Man Becoming*, p. xiv.

23. Ibid., p. 70.

24. Karl Rahner, *Opportunities for Faith: Elements of a Modern Spirituality*, trans. Edward Quinn (New York: Seabury Press, 1974), p. 66.

25. Ibid., p. 69.

26. Ibid., p. 71.

27. Baum, *Man Becoming*, p. 70.

28. Joseph M. Powers, *Spirit and Sacrament: The Humanizing Experience* (New York: Seabury Press, 1973), p. 27.

29. Ibid., p. 26.

7 New Morality as Discernment

To some people, New Morality spells lawlessness, paganism, and sexual license. One reason for their impression is that moralists today try to understand the meaning of all contemporary behavior and to reevaluate it, no matter what traditional categories dictate. But once we have begun this reexamination, we realize that however venerable some laws or principles are, they cannot survive if they fail to cope with life now or if they contradict or deny contemporary experience.

Moral Dialogue

New Morality puts law into perspective as the articulation of past experience, as part of traditional wisdom. It goes on to re-affirm the human resources beyond law: freedom, intuitive awareness, responsibility. It stresses that the basic moral experience is the inner Yes or No to life when we are confronted by demands of self, others, and the Other.

This may be another way to affirm that God did speak through situations and does continue to do so, that human history is then a network of human relationships immersed in Mystery Present. Each man, woman, and child is somehow hearer of the word. Primary revelation is always in the concrete set of relationships. Moral experts can contribute their share to the dialogue not only by refining and systematizing traditional moral thought, but especially by discerning and understanding our experience today.

This process of moral dialogue seems to have gone on with regard to Pope Paul's encyclical *Humanae vitae*. The outcry against this document in its teaching on artificial birth control marked the end of an era. Previously there had been the appearance of uniform direction and practice. But proclamation of the decree, coming after expectations had been raised, triggered the bomb that demolished the facade—to reveal ethical diversity and confusion.

One could object, of course, that resistance to the long-awaited *Humanae vitae* was a rebellion organized by traitorous theologians and professors. But this view seems an easy way to avoid the real issue, that armies of married people around the world had been helped to find their voice. And in effect what they said was:

> "Dear Holy Father, come on over here with us, where the *Church* really is on this crucial issue of family life. In every way we want to be as loyally Catholic and Christian as you. But our daily experience convinces us that accepting whatever children God sends was all right for our grandparents, but it's simply unworkable for us. In the privacy of our lives we discern what's right and wrong for today. You and your advisors made a big mistake. Admit it and please come."

This position was reached only after pain. As in all cultural shifts, it is the older people who have to study and struggle to accept plain facts that conflict with their upbring-

ing. I remember clearly the presentation by a Catholic couple
at a Better World Movement retreat some years ago. They
explained why they thought the official probition against
birth control was unrealistic and invalid. They readily understood how their married children could practice family limitation in good conscience. Yet they themselves, while convinced
intellectually, could not act against their nervous system:
they admitted they were using rhythm.

The *Humanae vitae* crisis served to clear the air, revealing how the worldview from an honorable but past era can be
inadequate to interpret experience today. Thus it is not impossible that, years from now, Pope Paul's decree may be re-
ferred to as another official document vividly recording
cultural change. Usury or money-lending, to take the standard example, was once declared immoral. Slavery was seen as
moral in 1454, when Pope Nicholas V defended the rights
of the Portugese to enslave "many people from Guinea as
well as other Negroes" in view of conversion.

DIALOGUE, DISCUSSION, AND DISAGREEMENT

New Morality, then, among other things, is today's effort
to read the signs of the times, to understand and interpret
our experience now. We are only claiming to exercise for
our times the prerogative which our ancestors exercised for
theirs. Whatever explicit moral conclusions we come to,
we want to arrive at them directly from real-life experience,
with a minimum of filtering through library shelves. True,
some people talk as if the dust will eventually settle on the
moral scene. Then, they say, Catholics at least can return
to the quiet normalcy of the recent past, when one knew
clearly what was right and what was wrong.

But wait, Curran warns, don't set yourself up for disappointment. Expect instead that "dialogue, discussion, and disagreement among Catholic moralists on methodological issues will continue to grow." Expect "to find continuing diversity in the search for more adequate moral theologies."[1] Not only is there no unanimity today on method or basic approach, but there are wide-open differences on particular issues. Where "previously there was *the* Catholic opinion," especially on marriage and sex, there is now for all to see "a divergence of opinions among Catholic moral theologians."[2]

That Catholic moral theology is shifting with the times is due to the fact that not only are the professionals debating among themselves, but also that they are listening to their clients, penitents, and friends.

Where this following of grass-roots experience will lead us is not clear. But we can imagine that in time professional moral theology — and eventually hierarchical statements — may put the seal of approval on behavior still outlawed by tradition, such as re-marriage "in the Church" after divorce. Serious debate is now going on whether there is scriptural and theological justification for continuing to forbid such marriages.

As adult Catholics reflecting on morality, we have to confront cultural shift and to accept realistic ways to interpret and evaluate our experience. We may even wind up approving tomorrow what we condemned yesterday — but no matter. We have to walk where our light leads. Fixity need not be the mark of authentic morality and religion.

The New Testament Jesus, apparently, was remembered as restless with mere observance of law, protesting, for example, that Sunday is for man but not man for Sunday. To meet the demands of the age (or, if you prefer, to heed the call of the Spirit), we may have to act beyond or against established rules, allowing them to fend for themselves. Vatican II did something like this in the area of doctrine; it faced today's issues squarely and, in fact, without planning to, made a quantum leap out of tradition, leaving to experts the thorny problem of how to preserve intact the notion of continuous doctrinal development from some original deposit of truths.[3]

What we are considering, actually, is the ineffable process of discernment, of finding out where the Spirit is blowing. That our reflections not be illusory, we test them in prayer and dialogue with others. But difference, tension, dissent, and even conflict will be inevitable. Professional moral theology follows as an effort to systematize and evaluate. Official statements follow professional reflection.

NATURAL LAW

Having been brought up tranquilly on certitudes and absolutes, Catholics particularly find the present situation threatening. For the classical theology of the recent past assumed a set of divine moral laws and principles that were to be applied to living as a blueprint. The laws and principles were thought to be eternal, certain, and unchanging. Somehow man could share the divine mind. Great trust was put in reason's capacity to deduce logically, from the moral absolutes in hand, all the concrete rules needed for daily conduct.

These moral absolutes were identified as natural law. But when applied to concrete situations, the natural law of the moral textbooks turned out to stress biological man. Hence condemnations of birth control, for example, said less about loveless family life than about the frustration of natural functions. The shift from classical worldview to contemporary is neatly characterized by Greeley: "Sex is between persons and not between organs."[4]

Recognizing that there is a perduring aspect of man, some moralists continue to use the term "natural law" but in a wide and dynamic sense. Macquarrie, for instance, sees a pattern of constant tendency in man. Natural law can be understood as "the pointer within us that orients us to the goal of human existence." Any rules, laws, and prohibitions are judged "by this 'unwritten law' in accordance with whether they promote or impede the movement toward fuller existence."[5] But the more static classical approach to natural law is no longer thought adequate.

> The concept of natural law as a deductive methodology based on eternal and immutable essences and resulting in specific absolute norms is no longer acceptable to the majority of Catholic moral theologians writing today.[6]

BIBLICAL ABSOLUTES

The Bible, of course, has been mined as a source of absolutes directly from God. But studies now show that the Ten Commandments, for example, were not unique to the Jews; their neighbors had similar codes of behavior. Furthermore, once you have an eternally moral absolute like "Thou shalt not kill," what can you do with it? Israel herself followed the tradition of holy war—not a grain of mercy to the vanquished. For the past two thousand years Christians have not in theory or in practice been a notably pacifist body. Crusades and burnings at the stake were acceptable at various times. In our day, Catholics have not been foremost in the movement to outlaw war or capital punishment. A great difficulty with any fixed rule, including presumedly divine absolutes, is that the exceptions begin to balloon out into sub-systems of their own, overwhelming the original taboo.

The Bible was used selectively, furthermore, to suit the cultural needs of any period. Thus a Hellenist or a Jansenist Christianity could cite Old Testament sex legislation in order to defend a celibate ideal already established among orders and clergy, whereas Judaism itself never saw celibacy as a value but only as a deprivation. The Old Testament does not promote non-sex as an ascetic ideal, nor were there Hebrew monks or nuns. Family life and fecundity were the norm.[7]

As for the New Testament, selectivity has been the common practice. One notable example comes from the history of Catholic theology. The minor metaphor *redemption* has colored the whole of Western doctrine—even though the term occurs less than twenty times, mainly in Paul. But the term *agape* or *love*, occurs over three hundred times in the New Testament—yet classical theology did not know what to do with it. Love is a non-logical, non-legal term pointing to personal relationship; it is best dealt with in poetry and in parables. The scholastic thinkers of the Middle Ages, and especially the official textbook writers of the past four centuries, put aside the troublesome idea of love to do the easier, rationalistic thing: they elaborated a strongly impersonal, legalistic, individualistic morality.

By contrast, Scripture scholars think that a morality in line with the New Testament tradition would be rooted in love of self, God, and neighbor. We are struck by "the charity-centeredness" of the early Church. "Christian moral life is a loving response to the prevenient love of God revealed in Christ and His saving deeds."[8] The recent revolution in

Catholic moral theology was Häring's restoration of the New
Testament to moral reflection. Contemporary Bible study,
for one result, stresses Mystery Present to us as invitation
and call through daily events. If there be a "Christian ethic,"
it would be less on the model of obeying law and more on the
model of call and response.

But we must be wary of behavior described as "Christian," as if it were something special or unique. People promoting causes too readily use the cliche, "This is the *Christian*
thing to do." On the level of deeds, anyhow, there seems no
marked difference between what good Christians do and
what good non-Christians do. "What is human," says Fuchs,
"is also Christian but not distinctively Christian."[9] On the
level of motivation, obviously, there can be a difference. But
"Christian morality in its categorical aspect," that is, on the
level of behavior, "is fundamentally and substantially human, hence a morality of authentic humanity."[10]

Curran would seem to concur: "In general I would opt
for a methodology in Christian ethics which is common to
the ethical enterprise and is not distinctive." This surely
would suggest that for the Catholic moralist "there remains
almost an infinite variety of such theories which one can
choose."[11]

What, then, does the New Testament add to moral reflection? Curran would respond by asking a more basic
question: How is a Christian different from other men? "In
my opinion this difference can at times be only the difference
between explicit and implicit." We could say that "The gospel
does make explicit, and explicitly Christian, what can be implicit in the consciousness of all men who are called by God."[12]
Everyone can be aware of goodness and Mystery; in the light
of the Gospel story of the Father's work in Jesus, Christians

believe that they have the most true and realistic interpretation of our religious and moral experience.

As for going to the Bible as the settled, direct dictation from the Lord on morality, Curran insists that "in no sense can the Scriptures be used as a book of revealed morality precisely because of the hermeneutic problem."[13] That is, as a collection of human testimonies, the Bible has to be read against its various historical contexts. It cannot be taken as a straightforward set of timeless absolutes. But even if we look at the differing moral orientations in the books of the New Testament, the general impression we come away with is that we are to solve our problems in a human way with human means, just as Jesus and the early Church worked at theirs. Morality that would be considered biblical or Christian would also be entirely human. What is moral is "that which is normatively human" or "that which is truly fulfilling of our humanity."[14]

One way to talk of this human morality is to describe it in dynamic terms: as a growing up, a coming out, a dying to self so as to live, a reaching beyond self to be oneself. Authentic morality cannot then be a mere conforming to some outside plan or code; it cannot remain a child's obedience to laws. Rather, it is a realization of free potential within, which follows a saying Yes to the divine we already are and which we experience.

"Morality implies human transformation," writes Baum, "entering into death to self-centeredness and receiving the freedom to rise to a new dimension of love." As we can see from the Father's work in Jesus, "human life is not a purely natural reality." It is always super-natural, for "God is redemptively present in the process by which man becomes more truly human."[15]

THE MAGISTERIUM

Thus far, then, we have located no clear-cut examples of moral absolutes (specific taboos, for instance) either in the natural law tradition or in the Bible. A third possible source could be the magisterium, usually understood as the teaching authority of the Church.

The teaching power of the pope has especially been thought of as guaranteed by infallibility. But once we examine the record of two thousand years, we cannot identify any moral absolutes proposed infallibly by pope, council, or bishop. We can assume that "there has never been an infallible, ex-cathedra pronouncement or an infallible teaching of the ordinary magisterium on a specific moral matter."[16] But then to expect church officials to be oracles without error, especially today with new and frightening moral issues posed by science and technology, is to caricature infallibility and magisterium. Maguire concludes "that the term 'infallible' does not in fact aptly describe the nature or function of the moral magisterium" and "that we should discontinue using that term" in describing it.[17]

In conclusion, then, there seem to be no moral absolutes from natural law, from the Bible, or from the hierarchical magisterium. Curran, for instance, counts himself among "an increasing number of Catholic theologians who deny the existence of negative moral absolutes; that is, actions described solely in terms of the physical structure of the act (a material piece of behavior) which are said to be always and everywhere wrong."[18] Apparently, therefore, when figuring out what is right and wrong in life, not only do we not have a whole positive program spelled out for us, but we do not have even one single taboo to go by which will be utterly unbreakable.

Our Moral Responsibility

The fact (whether harsh or joyful) is that we have to accept full moral responsibility: not only must we decide to do right but also we have to determine what is right in the first place. A part of being moral is taking the risk that we may be mistaken and wrong. It is immature to cling to presumed moral absolutes as an easy way to be safe by being sure.

But not to locate any moral blueprint is a very different thing from abandoning law or principle. There are journalists and writers of letters-to-the-editor who accuse theologians of doing away with law. In actual fact, no responsible moralist rejects law or laws. Perhaps characteristic are Maguire's rules about moral rules. First, trust them as "repositories of human ethical experience."[19] They preserve group wisdom and can serve as guidelines today. But secondly, distrust them. We should not be restricted to past insights.

Moral principles are helpful, then, in liberating us from having to reinvent ethics each time from the start. But no laws or principles relieve us of our responsibility. We cannot even appeal to so-called divine laws as having been directly given by God. It is men who have claimed to discern patterns in the universe that were attributed to God. Consequently, "divine" laws are actually man-made, just as all moral laws are man-made.

> That even rigid codes have been forced to admit exceptions and complexities should actually make clear that all moral rules are human artifacts. The fiction of divinely imposed rules does justice neither to the moral rules nor to God.[20]

Thus, for example, it has been traditional for Christians to say that mercy-killing is wrong because no man can presume to play God in deciding who will live or die, since God Himself has forbidden the taking of innocent life. Yet in other ways—as in ordering executions and in declaring war— down through history it is men who have defined and decided who these innocents will be. Despite the traditional language, in actual fact God never seems to have visibly or directly intervened in human affairs, and men never have ceased to "play God." For example, Columbus crossed the Atlantic, the National Aeronautics and Space Administration put men on the moon, and surgeons transplant kidneys.

We can handle our own affairs; for this purpose we were given portable brains. And we must handle them without abdicating responsibility. No Big Brother should be allowed to step in to relieve us of our privilege and duty to deal intelligently with tough issues like unemployment, world poverty, overpopulation.

Yet none of us is alone. There is evaluation and discernment, but it goes on in the various communities each person belongs to. Married couples must tell counsellors and moralists when they are not making sense. Moralists must urge economists and sociologists to further investigation of complex problems and to discover more creative alternative courses of action. This kind of dialogue has to be kept open, as the best that human beings can manage.

For there is never any guarantee that people will achieve the really right conclusions, the ultimate bedrock divine decrees. These remain veiled—in the event there are such things. All of us must feel our way in the murk. No person on earth has access to God's mind. No one has a hotline to Mystery, neither pope nor charismatic. Or, to reverse the image, each of us has a hotline of his own, with no individual or group possessing a monopoly. But in some way, collectively and individually, Mystery presides over mankind, as we fumble and take risks.

> We affirm that we cannot meet God alone, . . . that we cannot discover his divine will in solitude, because God is addressing himself to us as a family, as a community, in our togetherness and fellowship, even when the voice of his Spirit is necessarily moving and stirring the very core of the individual's heart and conscience. In other words, for God as well as for man, personal inspiration and corporate interpretation are two facets of the same reality of grace and charism.[21]

In such a Spirit-filled community, moral reflection can be seen as prophecy and dialogue. Prophecy is insight into and evaluation of the present. Official and natural leaders in the group call the community to appraisal and decision, without trying to specify or push particular responses. Dialogue is shared search. Prophecy and dialogue are the privilege and the responsibility of everyone. Actually, all are teachers and all are listeners.

This process is strikingly evident today in the systematic moral protests arising from concrete situations—the various liberation theologies. The five volumes of Segundo can be the model from the Third World. In North America we are experiencing a change of awareness because of pressure from the women's and gay liberation movements. When people perceive themselves as oppressed in some way, they begin to reinterpret life, including the traditional symbols of religion. Mystery Present is looked to as the God of a new exodus.

MORAL SENTIMENT

One element implicit in this community process is moral sentiment —each person's fundamental intuitive approach to judgment and action in life. In the past, perhaps, the laity were led to disregard this basic moral faculty. Thus, for example, the laity readily deferred moral issues to the confessor. Today, however, with greater numbers graduating from college and so on, there is less reliance on officials and experts. All in all, the laity are finding themselves and are appreciating their own profound resources.

Thomas Aquinas, for one, would understand. He distinguished two ways to come to correct moral judgment: first, by the use of reason and study; secondly, by a connaturality or feeling. For an example he takes chastity: "One who is versed in moral science will come to a right judgment through rational investigation, another who possesses the virtue of chastity will be right through a kind of instinctive affinity."[22]

Everyone can be aware of the ineffable process by which he comes to moral decision. Maguire stresses the value of such "affective perception of moral truth." He is convinced that it is "a palpable fact of life that very often the heart is wiser than the head when it comes to judging what is morally good." Obviously, "the heart can also be mean, self-serving, and dead wrong." But for various reasons, "ethics has all too often neglected the special contribution that our feelings and affections can make if we will pay them heed."[23]

Something similar is the faith-instinct identified by Rahner. This is each man's intuitive understanding of what he should do to be human, whether or not he can explain why in so many words. "The moral faith-instinct is aware of its right and obligation . . . even without going through (or being able to go through) an adequate process of reflection."[24] Even when we think we are acting on logically reasoned conclusions, we may really be proceeding on this instinctive judgment. Particularly when we are involved in situations that are complex, clouded, and shifting, it becomes clear that "conceptual analysis" will be "an essentially endless process." Then it is that this "universal moral instinct of faith and reason" allows us calmly to take risks, entering "into the darkness of reality (which is never completely transparent)."[25] Rahner would not base ethics on a deductive method that assumed we had some complete view of man from which we can safely draw out all the proper rules. Instead, he would begin with the discernment of Christians in the real-life moral decisions, trying in a later phase to articulate the reasonableness already in the decisions. Moral reflection, of course, follows decisions that men made spontaneously. Moral theology is an effort to systematize the intelligibility of what we do.

We need the officials and the experts—if only to assure us that we should trust our own judgments. But, as we saw in the case of *Humanae vitae*, professional moral reflection and official statements especially can lag behind grass-roots experience. Expectedly this is the case in times of cultural shift, when what was adequate for the fathers may not be sufficiently helpful for the sons.

DYNAMIC TENSION

There was a time, perhaps, when the process of moral discernment was simpler than now. The good Catholic checked with the rectory on moral matters, and the rectory consulted the manual of moral theology prepared by a Roman theologian. That method may seem superior to the conflictual process operating today—a process which invites change, confusion, plurality, dissent, even anger.

Nevertheless, the critical process may express faith and loyalty as much as the docile approach of the faithful in the immigrant Church, before Vatican II. On the theological level, anyhow, it can be argued that the conflictual process is a genuinely Christian way to discernment. It is a dynamic process involving everyone in the Church. For if the Spirit moves the community, each person will be impelled according to his or her gifts, and not in lockstep. As Rahner observes of a Spirit-filled community, there is "a multiplicity of impulsions," with the consequence that there is sometimes "a legitimate opposition of forces." Such opposition is not merely a necessary evil, but it must "be expected and must be accepted by all as something that should exist."[26]

The opposition may show up especially as a heightening of tension within the Church between "a divinely-willed dualism of charisma and office."[27] That is, in a dynamic church there is the hierarchical principle, which tends to conserve and control, and the charismatic principle, which tends to explore and criticize, to be creative and enthusiastic.

When it is a question of moral determination, the two elements could be classified as "ecclesiastical authority" and "the critical conscience of Christian people."[28] Both elements are legitimate, even when at odds. In theory, anyhow, there is no resolution to the tension between the two. Nobody in the Catholic Church really has the last word—only Mystery Present. Being neither a voting democracy nor a pyramid ruled single-handedly by a monarch, the Catholic community is instead "a society where no single authority holds all power combined."[29]

Today the lay people of the Church, after the long siege

of the Reformation, are discovering their place and power. Not mere sheep to be led, they too are teachers as well as listeners. To think with the Church is to be attuned to the various voices of all in the membership, which includes the officials. The phrase "The Church says" includes both laity and clergy. There are many magisteria.

As we are finding in our time, moral discernment can be a long and painful process, where good people may have to withstand each other, just as Paul stood against Peter at the first Church council on the issue of Jewish circumcision for Gentile converts. Tension can be expected especially in areas where "basic moral issues" touch the lives of "ordinary Christians such as religious liberty, social solidarity, peace and conscientious objection, ecumenical cooperation, responsible parenthood, etc." As Baum understands the interaction between the two principles,

> The Church is here dependent on the Christian experience of its people. When confronted with new moral issues, the Church has answers available only through sensitive and courageous Christian people who as believers discern the summons of the Spirit, discover guidance in their religious heritage, and engage themselves in faithful action. Theologians learn from these Christians. They test their action by submitting it to various critiques, and thus they help the hierarchy to exercise its pastoral office of teaching, guiding, clarifying, etc. But the process by which this takes place is conflictual.[30]

Even within a hierarchical Church, then, moral discernment is the duty and the privilege of each person. We are all responsible for each other, so that we cannot deny our share in moral dialogue today. But besides our Church community, we belong also to civic, social, and other communities, where we also share in dialogue. Private and public and international morality is too important to be left to moralists and churchmen, or to psychologists, economists, and government officials.

The times are changing, and whether we like it or not, whether we are ready for it or not, there is change in moral perception. "Where will it all end?" asks grandfather, as he looks up from the newspaper. But we should not fear where it will end. Mystery is present. What this means is effectively stated by Bishop Robinson: "what the new morality is saying to us . . . is that we need not fear flux: God is in the rapids as much as in the rocks, and as Christians we are free to swim and not merely to cling."[31]

NOTES

1. Charles E. Curran, "Moral Theology: The Present State of the Discipline" (Current Theology), *Theological Studies* 34 (September 1973): 454.

2. Ibid., pp. 456-457.

3. Cf. John W. O'Malley, "Reform, Historical Consciousness, and Vatican II's Aggiornamento," *Theological Studies* 32 (December 1971): 573-601.

4. Andrew M. Greeley, *The New Agenda* (Garden City: Doubleday, 1973), p. 142. The classical worldview, by contrast, is typified by this principle from Heribert Jone, *Moral Theology* (Westminster: Newman Press, 1961), p. 145: "The inordination [of sins of impurity] consists in one's seeking sexual pleasure . . . in a manner that frustrates the natural purpose of sex-life." A handbook in the vernacular, Jone's summary proved to be enormously popular in seminaries and rectories. The line above is from the English transla-

tion of the eighteenth German edition, which also appeared in five other European languages and in Arabic.

5. John Macquarrie, *Three Issues in Ethics* (New York: Harper and Row, 1970), p. 108.

6. Curran, "Moral Theology," p. 447.

7. Cf. Joseph Blenkinsopp, *Sexuality and the Christian Tradition* (Dayton: Pflaum, 1969).

8. Nicholas Crotty, "Biblical Perspectives in Moral Theology," *Theological Studies* 26 (December 1965): 593.

9. Josef Fuchs, "Is There a Specifically Christian Morality?" *Theology Digest* 19 (Spring 1971): 39.

10. Ibid., p. 40.

11. Charles E. Curran, "The Role and Function of the Scriptures in Moral Theology," Proceedings of the Catholic Theological Society of America 26 (1971): 80.

12. Ibid., p. 89.

13. Ibid.

14. Daniel C. Maguire, *Death by Choice* (Garden City: Doubleday, 1973), p. 77.

15. Gregory Baum, *Man Becoming: God in Secular Language* (New York: Herder and Herder, 1970), p. 132.

16. Curran, "Moral Theology," p. 457.

17. Daniel C. Maguire, "Moral Absolutes and the Magisterium," in *Absolutes in Moral Theology?*, ed. Charles E. Curran (Washington, D.C.: Corpus Books, 1968), p. 80.

18. Curran, "Moral Theology," pp. 454-455.

19. Maguire, *Death by Choice*, p. 90.

20. Daniel Callahan, *Abortion: Law, Choice, and Morality* (New York: Macmillan, 1970), p. 339.

21. Piet Fransen, "Hope and Anthropology: Is There Still Prophecy in the Church?" in *The God Experience: Essays in Hope*, ed. Joseph P. Whelan (New York: Newman Press, 1971), p. 154.

22. Thomas Aquinas, *Summa theologiae* II-II, 45, 2. Vol. 35, *Consequences of Charity (2a2ae. 34-36)*, ed., trans. Thomas R. Heath (New York: McGraw-Hill, 1972), p. 165.

23. Maguire, *Death by Choice*, 100.

24. Karl Rahner, "The Problem of Genetic Manipulation," *Theological Investigations*, vol. 9, trans. Graham Harrison (New York: Herder and Herder, 1972), p. 243.

25. Ibid., 239.

26. Karl Rahner, *The Dynamic Element in the Church* (New York: Herder and Herder, 1964), p. 73.

27. Ibid., p. 71.

28. Gregory Baum, "An Exchange of Letters," *The Ecumenist* 13 (November-December 1974): 14.

29. Rahner, *The Dynamic Element in the Church*, p. 71.

30. Baum, "An Exchange of Letters," p. 14.

31. John A. T. Robinson, *Christian Morals Today* (Philadelphia: Westminster Press, 1964), p. 20.

8 Psychology, Scripture, and New Morality

WHATEVER BECAME OF SIN? is Dr. Menninger's question.[1] So far as New Morality is concerned, there is still plenty of sin left, although the boundary lines may not be so easily drawn as once was thought.

LEGALISTIC VIEW OF SIN

In the classical moral theology of the recent past, "Sin is the free transgression of a divine law."[2] As this legal orientation showed up in the preaching tradition, sin was a matter of breaking commandments determined by God and Church. The textbooks and the handbooks on Catholic morality were organized within the framework of the Ten Commandments, as were the prayerbooks with their lists of questions for examination of conscience before confession.

But there are difficulties with such a view of sin. To begin with, it can be one-dimensional and shallow. To stress sin as transgression is to stress exterior behavior as separate, individual acts. Classification of sins becomes unduly important, and boundaries for sin become readily fixed. Such analysis leads one to think that it is easy to tell where the line is between virtue and sin, between venial sin and mortal.

Whereas in the Bible and in the great literatures, sin is something more profound and elusive. It is true that sin is talked about as keeping the law and minding the Commandments. But in the Old Testament, for example, sin is not merely breaking a law. Instead sin is "failing to conform to the covenant relationship that God had established between Himself and Israel." Biblical sin is a rupture of personal relation with God. "To sin is not simply to break a rule; it is to fail to respond to the love of Another."[3] Thus to insist today on the Ten Commandments as the basis of moral instruction, without insisting as well on the love or covenant context, is to miss the point of the Bible and to use the Commandments as another code of behavior.

A second difficulty with a legalistic orientation in morality is that it misses the pervasiveness of sin both within the individual and within society. To consider sin within the individual, we see it as something far deeper than simply not conforming to a law. Sin is profoundly one's stance on life. It is one's No to self, to others, to God. Sin is a real "dimension of man's life." It is, in dynamic terms, a "pathological resistance to growing up." It is staying afraid and mean-spirited within oneself. It is refusing interior calls and invitations—closing one's ears and shutting out the light.

> Sin is man's conscious and unconscious unwillingness to enter into new life, expressed and disguised in a multitude of ways, both personal and social; it opposes God's gracious gift of himself and thus prevents man from entering into his destiny.[4]

Sin is to not flow with our aspirations and nature, as Mystery urges us. Sin is rejecting openness, freedom, community, relationship.

A significant picture of personal sin in the New Testament is the parable of the Prodigal Son. In articulating his experience of reconciliation, the Son said less about wasting money on drink and women than about suspending relations with his father and with God. His sin was not presented as a series of individual transgressions, but as a sustained adventure in an alien land.

SOCIAL SIN

Sin is profound and pervasive not only within the individual but also in society. The story of Eden and of Adam's sin—apart from its being caught up in Augustine's notion of redemption—was one symbol pointing to our experience of the massiveness and mystery of evil in our daily human situation. A similar image from ancient literature is Pandora's box. The truth intended by the symbol of original sin is that all of human activity is interrelated, even if we imagine it, for purposes of analysis, as separate acts of distinct individuals. These presumedly separate acts accumulate and, so to speak, congeal into structures that pressure for evil as well as for good.

Structures causing evil can issue from activity evaluated as evil or sinful, but also from activity that may be harmless and even virtuous in purpose. And as we can see today, bright and well-intentioned people thinking that they were doing good perpetrated waste and carnage in the Vietnam war. Thus there are corporate crimes, governmental evils, ongoing economic injustices which may not be attributed to any particular bad persons.

History shows in abundance how even the silence of good people can contribute to unthinkable evil. One of the most appalling tragedies of history was the systematic slaughter of six million Jews in Nazi Germany, an attempt at genocide that went on practically without protest. Closer home has been the near extermination of the red race in America—at the hands of thousands of God-fearing people.

Current injustices flourish. The American citizenry seems generally aware that the tax system penalizes the poor and powerless, and only those who have money can hire the clever lawyers to save more money. In a country abounding with nourishing food, thousands do not receive an adequate share. And millions who have stamps and money for food, led on by furious advertising, stuff themselves with solids and liquids that are nonnutritious. On a planet soon to exhaust its oil reserve, we continue to buy oversized cars and each one of us millions drives alone to work. Junk yards and dumps, not to mention nuclear waste, are an increasing pollution problem. In a land of ingenuity, we do not seem to find any way to limit the sale of handguns. As much as anyone in our time, Ralph Nader has tried to be a prophet pointing to a national blindness regarding issues which are no less moral than they are commercial, economic, political.

Classical moral theology, it now appears, did not inspire questions for examination of conscience that got beyond one's individual situation. It did not sufficiently question the values of any group or of any economic and social system or of any culture. Yet these are the kinds of structures where, if anywhere, original sin is operating. If, for example, I want to help the farm workers under Cesar Chavez to secure their rights, I have to do more than be kind to my neighbor nextdoor. One thing that New Morality tries to do is to widen the scope of moral reflection, to understand and to raise our awareness of brutality, despair, exploitation weighing on all kinds of people on all levels throughout the world. To define sin simply as one's own transgression is to overlook enormous "social sins and corporate crimes that are based, not on free deliberation, but on false consciousness, on common blindness, on group involvement in destructive action in which people take part despite their good will."[5]

A further difficulty with classicial Catholic moral theology is its picture of God as lawgiver, on the model of king or emperor who issues law under sanction. This image of the divine obviously fit in with the monarchical systems of ages past. But when "ecclesiastical superiors understand their own authority in terms of jurisdiction including the power of coercion," they are naturally going to tend, "consciously or unconsciously, to present God as the supreme lawgiver who enforces obedience through divine sanctions." Such a symbol of God "protects the earthly authorities, ecclesiastical and secular." This lawgiver God was also "God the punisher." Motivational analysis further shows that this picture in the Christian imagination, "God as judge on a throne, meting out punishment, corresponds to a self-destructive trend of the human psyche."[6]

Meshing with this view of God is the view of man as fallen. Adam lost the Golden Age for us, so that we walk wounded on the earth today. All of this adds up to a pessimistic picture of life.

HUMAN INNER RESOURCES

Today, however, we Christians can shake ourselves free of such inhibiting images by reflecting on our own experience. We will, of course, not find everything pleasant there. For when we look into ourselves we become aware of dark pools inhabited by nameless possibilities. We can recognize ourselves in enormities presented dramatically in movies, TV shows, novels. Almost nothing, we candidly admit, is impossible to us. Yet when we are open to our own experience, we will also see a most encouraging part of ourselves—which religious tradition has not only neglected but purposely downgraded in the name of obedience, and especially of humility. In our time it is psychology that has been notably prophetic and healing, in so far as it warns us what to beware of and it helps us get in touch with our inner resources. To benefit from the empirical social sciences does not have to mean that we reduce morality to psychology and sociology.

Most remarkable, for example, is the fact that humanistic psychology seems to return us to the New Testament paradox of the Cross: to be ourselves, we must die to our smallness and greed, so that we can achieve our full self in the process of reaching out to others and being open to Mystery. Transformation follows death to our fearful, calculating, closed-up self.

Now it is possible that we do not find wholly creditable the more optimistic view of man suggested by our depths. Some of this reaction could be due to the fact that nearly all agencies in our life have not encouraged trusting our own organism. Neither school nor home. Then, of course, there was the dark view of man common to Christian churches both Protestant and Catholic. Whereas such a view of man is not shared either by the New Testament or by humanistic psychology. In the New Testament, we are temples of the Spirit. The kingdom of God is already here, among and within. Mystery is present. God is love. To our Father we are so important that even the hairs of our head are numbered. Especially in the transformation of the dead Jesus we can understand who we are and what we amount to.

In their own terms, professional psychologists tell a similar story. Carl Rogers, for example, after decades of clinical experience, is deeply convinced that man is an inevitably healthy being that wants to thrive and blossom. Each of us is an out-reaching organism, like "a pine tree" with "a leading tip which grows upward." Even when thwarted, it wants still to reach out. "In my experience in psychotherapy," says Rogers, "this forward thrust, this directional tendency toward wholesome growth, is the most profound truth about man."[7]

This inner push is toward the completion of the tree, but such completion means the very opposite of isolation. Our organism (ourselves as total self, as lumpy spirit) pushes toward self-completion, but this fulfillment in no way means isolation; to the contrary, we become and remain our best self only in reaching out to others. Hence Rogers observes that man is, "first of all, incurably social. It is my experience that man has a fundamental craving for secure, close, communicative relationships with others." And expectedly, man "feels very much cut off, alone, and unfulfilled when such relationships do not exist."[8]

Allport, for another, seems to crystallize our experience with this insight: "The truest statement that can be made of a normal person is that he never feels that he can love or be loved enough."[9] So that even if mankind according to the evolutionary worldview is emerging from the primeval muck with only partial success, we could still talk of life and "human nature" in terms of expansiveness, openness, freedom, community.

In the individual organism, failure to achieve growth and therefore relationship can mean illness. "We know," says Glasser, "that at the time any person comes for psychiatric help he is lacking the most critical factor for fulfilling his needs, a person whom he genuinely cares about and who he feels genuinely cares about him."[10] The science and art of psychiatry concerns the "two basic psychological needs: the need to love and be loved, and the need to feel that we are worthwhile to ourselves and to others."[11]

CHRISTIAN LOVE

One could object, of course, that this humanistic view of man is only that, a humanism. What has it got to do with *Christian* morality? But when we turn to the New Testament, we find no angelic or super-natural formula as the "Christian" way to be moral. Thus according to the parable of the Last Judgment (Matthew 25:31-46), we will be judged on whether we gave someone a drink of water, visited the sick, stood by a man in prison, attended a wake. The good Christian is one who gives first aid to someone robbed and beaten. The good Christian is a fully human person, who affirms your value and worth by actually listening to what you say. He is not trying (according to some recipe of the recent past) to "see Jesus" in you, but in a humane way he shares himself with you.

No matter what side we start from, then, our moral orientation and norm seem to come out much the same. If we claim to follow what the New Testament represents of Jesus and the first Christians, we will sum up the moral law under love of God, neighbor, and self.

If we look to the psychologists for cues, we will be invited to a "healthy openness to the mysterious" by men like Maslow.[12] The eternal question "Why are we here?" will be dealt with in terms of universal brotherhood, by men like Fromm: "The full answer lies in the achievement of interpersonal union."[13]

It may seem trite to recall that "the pivot of the Christian moral revolution is love," and that "the commandment of love . . . is the entire Christian moral code."[14] But this is the basic lesson that Christians have continually to relearn. This is what everyone else has to keep at also. But by the profession of their religion, Christians should be more completely committed to the task of concern for self and neighbor.

"He who loves his neighbor has fulfilled the law."[15] To love, in the New Testament, comes out as a strong imperative, fulfilling and eliminating the need for any other commandments. It is a command to do what by our very nature we really want to do anyhow: to feel our most free by being united with everyone we can. Yet we also dread to let ourselves go, so that we may in fact spend our lives sniping at others from behind our defenses.

The Christian program, then, seems an impossible ideal, even without adding the special reminder to love the enemy also. Hence a Christian less than any other should feel that he is good and chosen simply because of membership. The radical demand to love everyone allows no comfortable, self-satisfied Christianity. The Christian, in truth, has to be one who is willing to die for others—if he really is serious to do as Jesus did. Hence the haunting question: Who dares to claim that he is an authentic Christian? To recite a creed in unison at the assembly cannot be the final test of genuine religion.

Now this universal and unlimited love cannot be demanded if it has to be a tender feeling, or if we have to wait for the neighbor to love us in return. Yet, as Furnish shows, "the New Testament commendation of love is formulated in a *command* to love."[16] It can be a rigorous imperative because "love in the Christian sense is *not* something 'spontaneous,' but something which must be repeatedly called forth and repeatedly obeyed."[17]

"The love Jesus commanded" is to be taken "in just one way: as active goodwill toward the other." Such love does not depend upon the charm or intelligence of either party. My active concern for my neighbor is "my affirmation of him as a person who stands or falls quite apart from what I think of him." I may distrust and dislike him, but I care for him as "my acknowledgement of our common humanity."[18] The love command requires as a minimum that we live by our fellow-feeling.

Television especially has brought home to us the fact that planet earth is a global village. Today as never before we have some inkling as to what universal brotherhood can be. John Donne would have understood the thousands who marched against war:

> No man is an Iland, intire of it selfe; . . . any mans death diminishes me, because I am involved in Mankinde; And therefore never send to know for whom the bell tolls; It tolls for thee.[19]

Ironically, however, the agencies that should most foster brotherhood and sisterhood may in fact impede fellow-feeling. In the gospel Jesus is represented as proposing cases where religion can promote such a distortion. For instance, on a Sunday a neighbor's animal falls into a well. The law says we should do no physical labor on the holy day. Yet without hesitation we simply help our neighbor. The appeal that Jesus makes here, be it noted, is not to a sense of duty, nor to some higher law of charity, but simply to a sense of humanity (Luke 14:5). Then there is the story about the man robbed and beaten. Two churchmen passed up the victim lying along the road, for whatever reasons. But it remains my challenge to be compassionate, to be a feeling human being, to be the Good Samaritan.

Love of God and Man

The real sin, then—mortal sin if you will—is hardness of heart, passing people up, to give a stone to someone begging bread. This hardness is the opposite of metanoia or conversion, which Scripture experts see as the first moral duty outlined in the synoptic gospels. The Lord does not want our gift if we come with our hearts closed against any of His own, so that we have to leave our gift at the altar and first hurry back to be reconciled with our neighbor.

New Testament reflection comes out strong on love of neighbor as the touchstone of morality. Little or nothing is said about loving God directly apart from concern for neighbor. Not only is love of fellow humans our pledge that we can love God also, but there seems to be an identity.

According to the John tradition, agape or love is an overwhelming cosmic force flowing from God to man—not so that men can love God back right away, but so that we can share the love energy with each other. "No man has ever seen God," yet "if we love one another, God abides in us." Our experience will be of this hidden God present in human relationship. We are embraced by the all-encompassing dynamism of this Mystery Present, so that we are enabled to reach out to the people we live with. "In this is love, not that we loved God, but that he loved us and sent his Son to be the expiation for our sins." The conclusion here follows a new and Christian logic: "Beloved, if God so loved us, we also ought to love one another." The universe is a field of force, of vibrating love energy, which would draw us out to be ourselves most fully by our reaching out to everyone else. To hold back, through fear, greed, or whatever, is to block the cosmic dynamism that makes each being unfold and blossom. Furthermore, to say No to any fellow being is in effect to say No to the God who is love. "If anyone says, 'I love God,' and hates his brother, he is a liar; for he who does not love his brother whom he has seen, cannot love God whom he has not seen."[20]

Rahner argues how "it can really be said seriously that the love of God and the love of neighbour are one and the same thing."[21] He would maintain "that wherever a genuine love of man attains its proper nature and its moral absoluteness and depth, it is in addition always so underpinned and heightened by God's saving grace that it is also love of God, whether it be explicitly considered to be such a love by the subject or not."[22] Thus to flow with our fundamental fellow-feeling would be our ultimate integration. It is something like this that we admire in people who attempt great works, like Gandhi and Mother Teresa. He who loses himself in his neighbor finds himself, at the apex of consciousness and freedom. In this way the total love of neighbor would be "the one all-embracing basic act of human existence."[23]

That we complete ourselves in reaching out to others— the very opposite of remaining safe and cozy hiding under our rock—is affirmed by psychologists like Erich Fromm. To him, love is indivisible, an active orientation apart from love-objects. Our capacity to love reveals itself as a giving as well as a receiving—and a receiving that is not grabbing or possessing—rooted in our power to grow and expand. "Love is not primarily a relationship to a specific person." Rather, love is "an attitude, an orientation of character, which determines the relatedness of a person to the world as a whole, not toward one 'object' of love." It is really an openness "which refers to all and not to one."[24] Love is our Yes to the best we know, with a willingness to include all the goodness we could know. On the psychological level, we can see how there is no real distinction between being open to the Ultimate and being open to neighbor.

What confuses the discussion, of course, is the almost uncontrollable term love. It can mean so many things, some of them contradictory. A young couple, for instance, may talk about love, when in fact they are two immature and dependent people clinging. At its best, anyhow, love is a gift of self from a person standing on his two feet; in real life, of course, we do what we can, starting from wherever we are. It is interesting to note that Fromm describes love in concrete terms: "Love is the active concern for the life and the growth of that which we love." The basic elements of love are "care, responsibility, respect and knowledge."[25]

GENUINE SELF-LOVE

In all this, of course, to love others assumes proper respect and love for self. If the religious tradition of the West has faltered, surely it has been in the area of self-love. For various reasons, love of self became equated with selfishness. Today we can see better where the mistake is. Fromm makes the necessary distinction: "selfishness and self-love, far from being identical, are actually opposites." Clearly, "selfish persons are incapable of loving others, but they are not capable of loving themselves either."[26]

> The failure of modern culture lies not in its principle of individualism, . . . but in the deterioration of the meaning of self-interest; not in the fact that people are too much concerned with their self-interest, but that they are not concerned enough with the interest of their real self; not in the fact that they are too selfish, but that they do not love themselves.[27]

Christian asceticism has many lessons to learn from the psychologists. Western church tradition simplistically combated self-fulfillment, promoting a notion of humility and obedience that kept people docile to officials on all levels. Governments of both state and church that had a ruling caste tended to develop the theory of divine right. Any social system with an established elite will tend to keep the non-elite in their place by inducing the right self-image. The plantation system of the South would be an example. Today we are still trying as a nation to live with the consequences. "Black is beautiful" was a necessary stage of evolution for millions who had learned from youth, in ways both subtle and blatant, that they were supposed to be inferior.

> What is wrong with us and what causes the awful
> things we do, is not simply that we love ourselves
> too much but also that, on a deeper level, we do
> not love ourselves at all.[28]

In this regard, the psychological helping professions have spearheaded the movement to return people to themselves, to develop realistic self-esteem and sense of value. Not just the churches, of course, but Western competitive culture has led us to count our worth in terms of work, role, compensation. Who are you? "I am a student." Or "I am a secretary." An increasing number of people are accepting themselves as they are, so that they can just as readily identify themselves with "I am me." In general, however, the revolution in self-appreciation has only begun. It is most difficult for us not to think in competitive terms (successful versus unsuccessful, first place versus second, etc.). And it is difficult to neutralize our cultural stereotypes; sports and national heroes, for example, are expected to at least talk modestly if not self-deprecatingly.

Morality, then, can still be usefully summed up as love of self, of neighbor, and of Mystery. Insights from the empirical social sciences would seem to reinforce the New Testament tradition—a tradition which was not angelic or super-natural, but Semitic, earthy, and deeply humane.

The fundamental moral orientation we have looked at here, under the rubric of New Morality, seems to coincide with the fundamental faith orientation we dealt with under contemporary theology. Following the practice of classical theology, we still divide reflection on the big issues of life into doctrinal versus moral. But this division is only a convenience; we cannot say everything at once.

However, we must put the parts back together, after taking them apart for analysis. Thus as we see in our daily experience, to believe and to live rightly are rooted in an ultimate simplicity of attitude: an openness, the disposition to accept with our Yes. So that our moral stance is also our basic faith orientation. We say Yes—maybe with ease and joy, maybe with labor and pain—to the best we know. Our act of faith and our readiness to do right are expressed alike in our Yes to self, to others, and to Mystery Present.

All that theology and philosophy pick apart endlessly through the centuries can be experienced effortlessly in the daily life of a person saying Yes. "All these riddles would easily be resolved in the simplicity of any noble love," writes Chesterton of St. Francis of Assisi. "He was a lover of God and he was really and truly a lover of men; possibly a much rarer mystical vocation."[29] Knowing too well how we fear to abandon ourselves to Mystery and to others, we readily turn to make heroes out of people like Francis, in whom we see the courage and the joy to embrace the whole universe, without question and without reservation. This, we suspect, is really what it means to live.

NOTES

1. Karl Menninger, *Whatever Became of Sin?* (New York: Hawthorn Books, 1973).

2. Heribert Jone, *Moral Theology*, trans. Urban Adelman (Westminster: Newman Press, 1961), p. 46.

3. Eugene Maly, *Sin: Biblical Perspectives* (Dayton: Pflaum/Standard, 1973), p. 10.

4. Gregory Baum, *Man Becoming: God in Secular Language* (New York: Herder and Herder, 1970), p. 228.

5. Gregory Baum, "The Dynamic Conscience," *The Ecumenist* 12 (May-June 1974): 63.

6. Baum, *Man Becoming*, p. 223.

7. Carl R. Rogers, "A Humanistic Conception of Man," in *Science and Human Affairs*, ed. Richard E. Farson (Palo Alto: Science and Behavior Books, 1965), pp. 20-21.

8. Ibid., p. 20.

9. Gordon W. Allport, *Personality and Social Encounter: Selected Essays* (Boston: Beacon Press, 1960), p. 205.

10. William Glasser, *Reality Therapy: A New Approach to Psychiatry* (New York: Harper and Row, 1965), p. 12.

11. Ibid., p. 9.

12. Abraham H. Maslow, *Religions, Values, and Peak-Experiences*, (New York: Viking Press, 1964), p. ix.

13. Erich Fromm, *The Art of Loving* (New York: Bantam Books, 1956), p. 15.

14. John L. McKenzie, *The Power and the Wisdom: An Interpretation of the New Testament* (Milwaukee: Bruce, 1965), pp. 229, 230.

15. Romans 13:8.

16. Victor P. Furnish, *The Love Command in the New Testament* (Nashville, Abingdon Press, 1972), p. 199.

17. Ibid., p. 201.

18. Ibid., p. 195.

19. *Devotions Upon Emergent Occasions XVII* in *The Complete Poetry and Selected Prose of John Donne*, ed. Charles M. Coffin (New York: Modern Library, 1952), p. 441.

20. 1 John 4:10-12 and 20.

21. Karl Rahner, "Reflections on the Unity of the Love of Neighbour and the Love of God," *Theological Investigations*, vol. 6, trans. Karl-H. and Boniface Kruger (Baltimore: Helicon Press, 1969), p. 233.

22. Ibid., p. 237.

23. Ibid., p. 244.

24. Fromm, *Art of Loving*, pp. 38, 39.

25. Ibid., p. 22.

26. Ibid., p. 51.

27. Erich Fromm, *Man for Himself: An Inquiry into the Psychology of Ethics* (New York: Fawcett Premier Book, 1947), p. 143.

28. Baum, *Man Becoming*, p. 146.

29. G. K. Chesterton, *St. Francis of Assisi* (Garden City: Doubleday, 1924), pp. 21, 20.

Epilogue

In these eight chapters are the most satisfying theological insights that thus far I have been able to find for myself. I grew up with one set of religious views, but in time I felt obliged to doubt them, and finally to modify or replace them. Hence the questions I asked came not only out of my past but also in reaction to it, so that when I turned to professional theologians for help, I followed—of course not consciously at the start—certain principles of selection.

First, I applied the razor of the disillusioned. When one has been naive and overcredulous once, he does not want to be let down a second time. Confusion, dismay, and even anger are the feelings that we older Catholics may have to deal with. Having had to part with the overstuffed furniture, so to speak, I have since been content to use orange crates. This spareness may be evident in the section on Jesus particularly. I had lived through a phase of the American Catholic church when St. Paul's enthusiastic exclamations about Jesus were held up as the mark of authentic faith and when parish practices were a kind of Jesus religion. Hence when I began to question and to study, I found myself reacting against distortions and settling only for a rock-bottom minimum. The result is a chastened Christology. Other sections are likewise spare.

Second, I therefore went at theology with a sharpened sense of realism. There was no need to save face or form. Whenever we really do not know something, let's say so. Consequently, for example, if by any measure of communication God appears to be absent, let's face the fact squarely. Adopting this attitude, I was struck by the candor and realism of some contemporary writers, who on one hand affirm our ignorance yet on the other affirm the intimations in our depths. Such intimations, apparently, are as close as we can come to evidence for divine presence.

Third, starting randomly at study among courses and authors, only after some time did I realize that the people who really spoke to me were ranked as personalist and existentialist. Furthermore, without foresight or plan, the masses of notes I accumulated and the hours of listening and discussing seemed to fall aside, laying bare the one key notion of Mystery Present. This was a conclusion I arrived at, on the level of understanding—for I cannot pretend to have assimilated into my own life this wondrous approach. I see no reason, however, why I have to wait until I am an expert practitioner in prayer and politics before I share the good news. Obviously one could arrive at such a conviction after taking only an introductory course in theology, or after reading the New Testament—or apart from any reading or study. What is significant, however, is that after assiduous research, I refound a simple and elemental truth.

OTHER THEOLOGIES

In arriving at this basic insight, however, I considered various other possibilities. For example, I was exhilarated by the evolutionary vision of Teilhard de Chardin, influenced by fellow-students doing dissertations on him; yet I still do not know what to think of Teilhard's cosmic Christ. I had seen something, too, of the theologies of hope, but I did not find them compelling; while they exploit the promise and future aspect of the New Testament, they do not to me seem to make enough of present experience.

I also looked into one of "the most significant intellectual achievements of the twentieth century,"[1] an alternative to the classical worldview. This alternative is being elaborated by thinkers who are inspired by Whitehead's process model. Whitehead saw the universe as a vast unitary experience made up of nearly unlimited drops of temporal, interrelated experiences. In this sea of becoming, God is the supreme process, giving and receiving, ever changing and never completed, always persuading but never coercing. God alone is absolute, affecting each center of experience; He is supremely relative and temporal, being affected by all.

Whitehead boldly launched an original system when he proposed that we understand reality by generalizing "elements disclosed in the analysis of the experiences of subjects."[2] That is, from reading our awareness of self as the first instance of reality, we can better understand all reality by projecting our experience of self onto what is subhuman and onto what is divine.

In his analysis of self-experience, Whitehead discerned a mental pole and a physical pole. By its mental pole an actual entity grasps possibilities, and by its physical pole it realizes them concretely. When extrapolating this dipolar process model, Whitehead discerned a dipolar process God. God's mental pole (His primordial nature) presents conceptually to each unit of process the range of possibilities to be realized. The process God is therefore "not *before* all creation, but *with* all creation."[3] He is present as attracting and luring. God's physical pole (His consequent nature) is wholly involved with the flux of the world, being acted upon through the decision of each drop of experience. As consequent, God is temporal and changing, the recipient of all that has happened in the order of creation. With his dipolar God, Whitehead aimed to integrate change and permanence, time and eternity, finity and infinity. He hoped to establish a worldview that would correct the deficiencies of a classical tradition, according to which the world was a warehouse of separated, static substances suffering accidental changes, and where God was an absolute monarch beyond reach.

Hartshorne especially has used the process model to avoid the contradiction of classical theology, according to which reality at its best is completion and perfection, while becoming, time, and motion are symptoms of limitation. In such a worldview, the supremely perfect being is the Unmoved Mover of Aristotle, who is wholly unaffected by anything outside of it, and who finds only himself as the proper object of thinking and loving. But then who can pray to this unmoved kind of deity? So far as Christians adopted the classical assumption of a Supreme Being with a one-way relation to creation, they have never produced convincing reasons for prayer. To defend their actual practice, they have to be inconsistent and to take refuge in the Bible.

There are definite advantages, then, in adopting the process worldview, starting with the fact that it proves to be a most elegant contemporary model, more or less adequate to the demands not only from theology and Scripture but also from physics, mathematics, aesthetics, and so on. An increasing number of writers employ the process model. Because of its comprehensiveness, Barbour proposes that the process model be "given priority" over others,[4] even though we realize that no one system can supply the final language to express "the experience of the Christian com-

munity."[5] Having identified five basic modes of theologizing, Tracy does not hesitate to propose process theology as
the best kind for modern man.[6]

We have taken up process theology in some detail here,
since it affords a strikingly instructive example of how a
theology can get started and what theology can be. Clearly
the process model is a man-made option that is developing
under our very eyes. No set of theological symbols, of
course, is ever anything other than man-made. Whitehead is
particularly candid in remarking that in his discussion of
God, "there is nothing . . . in the nature of proof." All we
have is "merely the confrontation of the theoretic system with
a certain rendering of the facts." Such facts include the
"somewhat exceptional elements in our conscious experience." But even the process model used to elucidate our experience is "confessedly inadequate."[7] Thus even though
Whitehead may seem to talk confidently of God as "the
great companion—the fellow-sufferer who understands,"[8]
he still insists that whatever he says about God "cannot be
looked upon as more than suggestions."[9]

There is, of course, no way for us to get at the deep-down
facts of the situation. Is God really an unmoved hearer of
prayers—or, rather, an unmoved nonhearer? Or is God really
in dialogue with men and nature—like the Yahweh of the
Jews and the Father of Jesus, or like the Process God? We
are here dealing only with what we believe and not with
anything anyone can actually prove or inspect.

Now, obviously, despite the excellencies of process
theology, I did not opt in these chapters for the Whiteheadian
model. This was a deliberate choice. The fact is that at one
time I examined Whitehead's works closely and even had
begun a dissertation on Whitehead's God. I suppose, however, that I lost interest as it became clearer to me how in

the process worldview a human being is a colony of actual entities. That sort of visualizing may be congenial to people with mathematical or scientific mentalities (Whitehead was an eminent mathematician); but the process model, I would think, speaks only to certain kinds of people.[10] I myself feel comfortable only with dramatic images when reflecting on life and the world.

Furthermore, process thinkers make much of the fact that their work coincides with the Jewish and the Christian scriptures. But the Bible deals with all the life-and-death issues in dramatic terms. The Ultimate is thought of as a supreme person who carries on a dialogue with men. Even for us today, the New Testament pictures of a kind Father can suffice as an answer to the question: How can God relate to creatures? I myself am content to leave the analysis at that, without going into the two-pole conjecture that some find helpful.

Our choice of worldviews is not restricted, then, to the dilemma: either the Process God or else the Unmoved Mover. We can choose to employ the images of human drama from the everyday macroscopic world. This book has consistently used the "interpersonal model" or "the dialogic model" to suggest our relations to Mystery Present. This is of course the common model of the Bible. It is the model of existentialists like Buber and Bultmann, who stressed the I-Thou character of "the interaction of God and man in the present moment."[11]

More than any other model, the interpersonal seems able to articulate what is of prime importance in theological reflection: our depth experience. To deal realistically with such experience seems the first criterion for valid theological insight. For our depth experience embraces all the hints

and glimmerings that alert us to the religious and transcendent dimension of life, which we examined in chapters two
through six above. But as we saw under New Morality, depth
experience embraces also our fundamental fellow feeling,
so that we are aware of some kind of continuity between
Mystery Present and neighbor and ourselves. To express
these ineffable relations only the dialogic or personal model
seems adequate. By contrast, process theology (at least if it
is systematic) seems overly intellectual and technical. In
fact, professional theology in general tends to be occupied
with the tidiness and elegance of its model, so that system
can become a ruling consideration.

THE LIMITATIONS OF PERSONALIST THEOLOGY

When we opt for a stance that is strongly personal and experiential, however, then we also have to recognize its limitations. For one thing, "The dialogic model makes a sharper
separation of man and nature than can be justified today."
The theory of evolution and our heightened awareness of
ecology have shown us the continuity and relation between
human and subhuman. We could so concentrate on our in-
ward relation to Mystery Present that we forget the meaning of nature and its relation to God. Nature becomes
something to exploit. "Today we need a theology of nature
as well as of human existence."[12]

But there can be a more grave problem with a personalist
theology. The issue is clearly expressed in a foreword that
Metz did for a book by Rahner. He appreciates Rahner's
theology for its "one overriding tendency: the ever new
initiation into the mystery of God's love and the service of
the hope of all men." Yet when we adopt a model focusing
on the individual's free Yes, "Is there not danger that the

question of salvation will be made too private and that salvation history will be conceived too worldlessly?"[13]

Left to itself, personalism could focus on love for God
as a one-to-one relationship. A personalist theology could
thus be taken as reinforcing the ghetto view of church, one
which shelters its children and avoids involvement in social
issues. This could mean that a person hoping to renew himself today by shifting from the classical worldview to that of
some contemporary horizon could in fact leave the individualism of the recent past (Jesus-and-me) for a contemporary
individualism (Mystery-and-me).

We have to be aware of our individualistic traditions. As
Christians of the West we were brought up on individual
conversion and decision for Jesus, and on individual salvation. Besides that there is our individualistic' American
heritage: private enterprise by which we compete in order
to achieve the isolation of private automobiles, private tele-
visions, private clubs, and so on. The New England inherit-
ance of Emerson's self-reliance moved westward as the myth
of a Shane, for instance, the gunman hero who rights the
wrongs of a settlement and rides out of town as alone as when
he arrived.

We have a long and strong tradition of individualism,
therefore. So that when we try today to renew ourselves and
society, we have to recognize our "tendency to reduce the
heart of the Christian message and the practical exercise
of faith to the decision of the individual standing apart from
the world."[14] Even the New Testament can be taken in a
highly private sense. Bultmann, for instance, has taught
theologians how to ask the existentialist question: What
meaning can this Gospel text have for decision in my life?
But no matter what our background, when we read the parable of the Good Samaritan, we all readily understand it on a

privately personal scale: morality is how I treat this or that individual.

PERSONALISM AND SOCIAL RESPONSIBILITY

Personalist theology, then, can be severely criticized for allowing such shortsightedness and distortions. Nevertheless, there is no inherent relation between individualism in religion and the employment of the dialogic model. There was certainly no problem in the Old Testament, where the dialogue was not between God and me, but between God and His people. The political theologian Sölle shows that the New Testament also bears a universal interpretation and not chiefly a private one. Today, for example, we would be justified in translating the parable of the Good Samaritan into a story about effective social action. Not only would the Samaritan give first aid to the victim left by the roadside, but he would change the structures that produce victims. Translated into movie terms, he would form a posse and go at once to clear the robbers out of the forest. Or, better yet, taking a leaf from Saul Alinsky, he would elicit grassroot interest and organize groups and coalitions that pressure city hall to provide better street lights and more police power.

Metz in particular has proposed a "political theology" as "a critical corrective of a certain tendency to confine theology to the realm of the private and personal."[15] It is no accident that political theology issues from Germany, where for a generation Bultmann has been a strong influence. Nevertheless, if a corrective is needed, and even a massive one, it does not seem necessary to establish what appears intended as a new brand of theology. In fact, to develop a distinctive "political theology" could be a way to cut the social side of theology off from its roots. It seems to create a false dichot-

omy, as if we now have to choose between political theology
and personalist theology (dialogical, mystagogical, existen-
tial).

There seems to be a great need for personalist categories,
not for themselves but because they seem the best way to
express what is crucial for theological reflection: the religious dimension of our human experience. It would be a
great loss, then, to promote a political theology—whether
American or German—if the new emphasis were to down-
grade the importance of depth experience.

LIBERATIONIST WORLDVIEW

There seems less danger that depth experience will be swal-
lowed up in the liberation theologies. In a work that is a
prime example from the Third World, Gutierrez charac-
terizes "the theology of liberation" as an attempt "to reflect
on the experience and meaning of the faith based on the
commitment to abolish injustice and to build a new society."[16]
Scharper sums up much that is being done: "theologians of
liberation have attempted to read the Scriptures through
the prisms of the poor."[17] The oppression widely experienced in Latin America is economic, political, and social.
The theologies of liberation articulated in North America
are responses from women rejecting sexist oppression and
from blacks rejecting racial oppression. So far as these protests are theological, they can be considered "an elaboration
of political theology or theology of hope,"[18] but while a
theology of hope can become a strongly academic study of
scriptural texts, the liberationist reinterpretation of the
Bible remains in close contact with daily living.

Thus groups becoming aware that they are victims of
society reflect on traditional religious symbols in order to

discover readings that express their feeling of outrage, of compassion, of solidarity in fellowship. Depth experience can be as readily articulated in solitary prayer and public worship as in efforts to remove unjust structures and to establish better ones. Mysticism and action are correlatives.

> Believers encounter the divine by involving themselves in the struggle for humanization. Since the transcendent mystery is operative in the promised transformation of human life, personal and social, it is here, in *active* engagement and *contemplative* presence to this engagement, that believers encounter the living God.[19]

Obviously for our time it is not easy to determine a good balance between contemplation and action. It was easier in the past, when we relegated contemplation to nuns in cloisters. It is not a simple lesson for us to learn that we can no longer slight our depths, that action without mysticism is building on sand. Thomas Merton explored such issues for modern man. In a study of Merton's thought on the matter, Kelly concludes: "Merton was convinced, from his personal experience, that it was necessary for religious man to find his true self in God before he could become socially involved."[20]

That the private side of life has to be respected at all cost, no matter what the scope of public life turns out to be, is indicated in an interesting test case. The well-known Spiritual Exercises of St. Ignatius are highly individual. So in order to make them more relevant should the Jesuits and their retreatants now relocate in the inner city? Father Byron, a sociologist, has this to say: "It would be a mistake, I think, to permit the Ignatian retreat experience to move away from the private (physical withdrawal) and personal (solitary prayer under the guidance of a personal director) in an ef-

fort to enhance social awareness or deepen social commitment." Even if solitary prayer were not valuable in itself and
useful only as preparation for action, it would be still "in the
'Apartness' of the guided prayer experience that social consciousness can deepen."[21]

As for finding our way through social issues today, we
are all pioneers in an uncharted area. It was easier in the
past, when our neighbor was the person next-door. Even if
we treated him unjustly, at least we knew with whom to be
reconciled. But today, now that we are beginning to realize
the power and pervasiveness of social sin, we cannot see
clearly whom we are hurting nor how. Even by being faithful to our daily duty, for example, we can perpetuate economic systems that keep whole groups powerless and poor.
Not to protest can be to permit injustices to continue. Thus
the grape and lettuce boycotts against agribusiness growers
added decisively to the pressures that finally forced recogni-
tion of the farm workers.

But once we inaugurate this kind of social conscience examination, there seems no end to the issues. Liberationists at
home and abroad leave us very little margin for a contented,
comfortable middle-class Christianity. We are like the main
character of *The Fall* by Camus. On a bridge late one night
in Paris, Clamence saw a woman leaning over the railing.
Having crossed the bridge, he heard a splash and loud cries.
But he did not run back to the bridge, he did not call the
police, and for days afterward he avoided newspapers. He had
succeeded in closing his eyes and ears, but he could not
shut out his memory: haunted by his crime, he spent his
days in a bar confessing his sin to the customers.

Something akin to this guilt is experienced today by
some people. One among this increasing number of concerned Christians is Richard Shaull. As a missionary in

Latin America for twenty years, he helped develop libera-
tion awareness and theology. But he has returned to the
United States to declare: "I am a white, middle class, male,
North American."

> If I have learned anything in recent years, it
> is that authentic theological reflection cannot be
> imported. If we want to think theologically about
> liberation, then it is *our own liberation* that must
> concern us. . . .
>
> I, a constructor of prisons for most of the rest
> of the world, am myself a prisoner. In fact, I have
> helped actively to build the walls which imprison
> me; I have allowed others to build these prison
> walls around me without any strenuous objections
> on my part.[22]

Shaull proposes no programs, but he recommends that people
who have come to question their part in building an unjust
world could find mutual support in discerning what now to
do—by forming communities.[23]

In our day, the era of the supermarket, we have achieved
the golden age that Renaissance men like Descartes hoped
and worked for—the time when machines and not men would
hew wood and draw water. But the benefits of technology
are not evenly distributed, nor the conditions for dignity
and humanity. Even in the world's richest country perhaps
forty million persons classify as poor. In a stratified culture
of ages past, such a situation might have been accepted as
predestined and natural. Today, however, poverty and
indignity are taken as evils to be abolished. Such a change
on the face of the earth is not to be brought about through
acts of benevolence by individuals, but only through social

and political agencies. To drop off a Christmas basket with a poor family is obviously no longer enough; we might achieve something more helpful and lasting by joining a picket line. In our age of new social awareness, the very preaching of "the Gospel, precisely insofar as it is a message of total love, has an inescapable political dimension."[24] That is, there can be no authentic love of self or love of God unless there is also a realistic, nitty-gritty concern for our neighbor. This is a new understanding of an old principle in Christianity, that charity has to be concrete and historical.

But how to translate gospel love into plans for action is a problem that even the practical liberation theologies do not seem to deal with successfully. Actually, there can be no clear conceptual path from the Christian love commandment to its social and political implications. There is no way to bypass the labor of mastering disciplines like economics and sociology. So that the most that liberation theologies can derive from the New Testament is a new reading. But we cannot wait for the final liberationist interpretation of traditional symbols.

Nor do we need to wait, for we rely on our inner resources, our depth experience. On the psychological level—even if we do not succeed in articulating the theology of it—we experience the continuity from self, to all men and women, to the Unlimited. This is our experience of love in the large sense: "an attitude, an orientation of character, which determines the relatedness of the person to the world as a whole." It is really an openness "which refers to all and not to one."[25] To love is to embrace all and to hang on to nothing. This is the astonishing, luminous force we claim to see in St. Francis of Assisi. Something of this we discern in people today who put themselves on the line for a better world. To say the total Yes to ourselves, to each other, and to Mystery Present is to stand before the world — and before our own mirror — totally liberated.

Whatever the kind of oppression a liberation theology would take off from, its reflections would eventually have to get into the issues dealt with in these eight chapters. If we ever evolve a liberation theology for us white, middle class North Americans, it will have to take full account of depth experience and Mystery Present and genuine self-love and practical concern for neighbor.[26]

To conclude, I must return to the aim of the book: to share my experience with those who are also asking questions. I am not out to challenge the convictions of anyone. I respect those who understand their fidelity to the faith as keeping unchanged what they may have learned in childhood. My testimony may be helpful to those searching for better explanations. Since I am neither a professional nor a life-long theologian, I had to begin at the beginning, with a layman's frustrations and perplexities. I cannot claim to have the answers, nor to be right. But until church spokesmen and theological experts offer us more immediately helpful things, I feel that there is a place for me to tell my story.

NOTES

1. Schubert M. Ogden, *The Reality of God and Other Essays* (New York: Harper and Row, 1966), p. 56.

2. Alfred North Whitehead, *Process and Reality: An Essay in Cosmology* (New York: Social Science Book Store, 1929), p. 252.

3. Ibid., p. 521.

4. Ian G. Barbour, *Myths, Models and Paradigms: A Comparative Study in Science and Religion* (New York: Harper and Row, 1974), p. 166.

5. Ibid., p. 170.

6. David Tracy, *Blessed Rage for Order: The New Pluralism in Theology* (New York: Seabury Press, 1975), pp. 172-203.

7. Whitehead, *Process and Reality*, p. 521.

8. Ibid., p. 532.

9. Ibid., p. 521.

10. We do not have, of course, to adopt the Whiteheadian system in order to exploit key process insights such as: the interrelatedness of everything, the ongoingness of creation, our interaction with God and the depth of our freedom, God's initiative and share in our becoming. See, for example, Bernard Lee, *The Becoming of the Church: A Process Theology of the Structures of Christian Experience* (New York: Paulist Press, 1974).

11. Barbour, *Myths, Models and Paradigms*, p. 157.

12. Ibid., pp. 157-158.

13. Johannes B. Metz, "Foreword" to *Spirit in the World* by Karl Rahner, trans. William Dych (New York: Herder and Herder, 1968), pp. xvii-xviii.

14. Johannes B. Metz, "Political Theology," in *Sacramentum Mundi: An Encyclopedia of Theology*, vol. 5, ed. Karl Rahner et al. (New York: Herder and Herder, 1970), p. 35.

15. Ibid., 35.

16. Gustavo Gutierrez, *A Theology of Liberation: History, Politics and Salvation*, trans. Caridad Inda and John Eagleson (Maryknoll: Orbis Books, 1973), p. 307.

17. Philip J. Scharper, "The Theology of Liberation: Some Reflections," *Catholic Mind* 74 (April 1976): 45.

18. Letty M. Russell, *Human Liberation in a Feminist Perspective — A Theology* (Philadelphia: Westminster Press, 1974), p. 20.

19. Gregory Baum, "The Christian Left at Detroit," *The Ecumenist* 13 (September-October 1975): 91.

20. Frederic Joseph Kelly, *Man Before God: Thomas Merton on Social Responsibility* (New York: Doubleday, 1974), p. 265.

21. William J. Byron, "Privatization—A Contemporary Challenge to Ignatian Spirituality," *Chicago Studies* 14 (Fall 1975): 244.

22. T. Richard Shaull, "Grace: Power for Transformation," in *Liberation, Revolution, and Freedom: Theological Perspectives*, ed. Thomas M. McFadden (New York: Seabury Press, 1975), pp. 76, 77.

23. Ibid., p. 81.

24. Gutierrez, *A Theology of Liberation*, p. 270.

25. Erich Fromm, *The Art of Loving* (New York: Bantam Books, 1956), pp. 38, 39.

26. Baum would say that "Theologians of the dominant culture in America are unable to produce a liberation theology." They can develop only a "critical theology" or a "theology of captivity." Baum, "The Christian Left at Detroit," p. 98.

Index

Adam, 11, 21, 57, 58, 59, 60, 61, 98, 131, 133
Alinsky, Saul, 155
Allport, Gordon, 135
Anselm of Canterbury, 59, 60
Aquinas, Thomas, 25, 29, 32, 122
Aristotle, 150
Atheism, 18, 44
Augustine of Hippo, 20, 43, 60, 61, 78, 131

Baptism of infants, 11, 20-21, 57, 60, 67
Barbour, Ian, 150
Baum, Gregory, 12, 33, 43, 53, 117, 125
Bible: as culturally conditioned, 17, 19, 26; as expression of community faith, 27; as human literature, 27, 117; in metaphorical language, 16, 30, 62-65, 115; as moral source, 114-117; not divinely dictated, 22, 26, 28, 30, 117; as picture of Jesus, 19, 26-28; as secondary revelation, 100-101
Brotherhood, universal, 14, 53, 87, 99, 105, 138
Brown, Raymond E., 68
Buber, Martin, 152
Bultmann, Rudolf, 152, 154, 155
Byron, William J., 157

Callahan, Daniel, 29
Camus, Albert, 18, 158

Change: cultural, 16-17, 20, 110, 123; ecclesial, 20, 23, 73, 76; moral, 77-78, 110-113, 123, 126; theological, 11, 13, 16-17, 21, 23, 57-66, 73, 78-79
Chavez, Cesar, 132
Christianity. *See* Church, Christian
Church, Catholic: authoritarian past of, 31, 73-76, 92-93, 133; cell model of, 84-86; charismatic vs. hierarchical in, 31, 91-93, 123-126; conflict in, 20, 112-113, 123-126; ecumenical approach of, 78-79, 81-82, 83-84, 103-104; identity today of, 47, 48, 81-82; institutional model of, 31, 74-76, 124, 133; magisterium of, 12, 22, 23, 28, 31, 75, 118, 120-121; reliance on right words in, 15, 19, 25, 31, 45, 92; Spirit in, 17, 20, 53, 124; transition period of, 20-21, 58, 73, 76. *See* Church, Christian
Church, Christian: based not on words but on Spirit, 20, 28, 124; centers on religious experience, 45, 51, 93-95; as community of Mystery, 47, 53, 85-87, 95, 97; distinct from kingdom, 79-80; Easter faith of, 14, 19, 20, 27, 38, 47, 64-65, 66, 82, 84, 99, 115, 117, 134; election, motive of membership in, 80; explicitness as distinctive of, 48, 81-82, 104, 116-117; main message of, 47,

137-138, 140, 153, 157; no direct divine intervention in, 12, 117, 119-120; role of moral experts in, 109, 113, 118, 120-121, 123, 125-126; role of laity, 110, 119-126
Moral responsibility, 119-121, 123-126
Morality: biblical, 114-117, 136-140, 143; Christian aspect of, 115-117, 136-140; classical, 129-130, 132-133; conflictual method of, 110-113, 123-126; contemporary, 109-111, 126, 129, 132, 143, 153; humanistic aspect of, 116-117, 133-136, 143; identical with faith, 14, 68, 69, 95-96, 101, 109, 117, 143, 160-161; as love of self, neighbor, God, 14, 54, 109, 115, 136-143, 153; norm of, 116-117; principles and law in, 109, 113-114, 119; as risk, 119-121; as saying Yes, 37-39, 68, 69, 97, 99, 109, 117, 143, 160-161; socio-political aspect of, 53-54, 86-87, 97, 157, 158-161. *See* Faith; Love; Moral discernment
Moran, Gabriel, 47, 84, 86
Mystery and wonder, sense of, 25, 31, 32, 36, 51, 95
Mystery Present: affirmed in faith, 36-39, 68, 69, 78, 116-117, 143, 160; celebrated in liturgy, 51-52, 53, 82, 101-105; as creator, 97-99; experienced as intimations, 33-36, 43; as liberating force, 97, 121, 130, 160-161; as main message of Christianity, 47-49, 54; as major motif of contemporary theology, 13, 32, 39, 43, 47-49, 54, 93, 95; meaning of the term, 13, 36; as moral inspiration, 116, 120-121; as primary object of Christian

life and worship, 46-49, 53; as redeemer, 64-66, 77, 98, 99; as salvation and savior, 77, 99. *See* God the Unknown Father; Mystery Present, devotion to
Mystery Present, devotion to: communal aspect of, 53, 85-87; as identity of Christian, 47-49; individualistic trend in, 52-54, 115, 132, 141-142, 153-155; Jesus as mystagogue, 45; liturgy as, 51-52, 82, 102-105; mystagogy as, 39, 43-45, 50-54, 91-96, 157; socio-political implication of, 53-54, 86-87, 97, 157, 158-161. *See* Mysticism
Mysticism, 39, 43-45, 91-96, 157. *See* Experience, depth

Nader, Ralph, 132
Natural law, 113-114
New Morality, 109-111, 126, 129, 132, 143, 153

Original sin, theory of: challenged by Bible experts, 11, 57-61; challenged by science, 11, 57, 58; developed by Augustine, 60-61; difficulties with, 11, 21, 57-62; as symbol for social evil, 62, 131, 132-133

Paul of Tarsus, 17, 19, 61, 67, 77, 80, 92, 115, 125, 147
Paul VI, 110, 111
Personalist model. *See* Theology
Peter, 27, 64, 77, 125
Peter, Carl J., 80, 102
Powers, Joseph M., 104
Prayer, 47, 49-54, 82, 150-151, 157-158
Political theology. *See* Theology
Process theology. *See* Theology
Prophecy, 85, 87, 97, 121, 132, 155,